RICHMOND *Handbooks*

C000177110

Series Editor : Paul Seligson

Developing
Resources
for
Primary

Amanda Cant and Wendy Superfine

Richmond PUBLISHING

Richmond Publishing
19 Berghem Mews
Blythe Road
London W14 0HN

ISBN: 84-294-5066-1
Depósito legal: M-9.357-1997
Printed in Spain by
Palgraphic, S. A.

Design   Jonathan Barnard
Layout   Gecko Limited
Cover Design Geoff Sida, Ship Design

Illustrations   Gecko Limited, John Plumb, Liz Roberts

Contents

Richmond Handbooks for Teachers: An introduction

This series presents key issues in English Language Teaching today, to help you keep in touch with topics raised in recent educational reforms. The books all contain a mixture of analysis, development work, ideas and photocopiable resources for the classroom. The key note throughout is what is **practical**, **realistic** and **easy to implement**. Our aim is to provide a useful resource which will help you to develop your own teaching and to enjoy it more.

While each of the books has been written for the practising English Language Teacher in the primary or secondary environment, they are also suitable for teachers of languages other than English, as well as for teachers of young adults, trainee teachers and trainers.

All classroom activities are designed for lower-level classes (from beginners to lower intermediate) as these form the majority of classes in both primary and secondary. Most of them can, however, be easily adapted to higher levels.

The books all contain:

- *a section of photocopiable activities and templates.* These are either for immediate classroom use (some with a little adaptation to suit your classes) or for use throughout the year, e.g. assessment record sheets or project work planners.

- *regular development tasks.* These ask you to reflect on your teaching in the light of what you have just read, and some ask you to try new ideas in the class. They are all intended to make the ideas in the books more accessible to you as a classroom teacher.

- *an index of activities.* As most teachers dip into or skim through resource books, there is an index at the back of each book to help you find the sections or ideas that you wish to read about.

- *a comprehensive glossary.* As one of the main principles of the books is ease of use, the authors have tried not to use jargon or difficult terminology. Where this has been unavoidable, the word/term is in SMALL CAPITALS and is explained in the glossary at the back. Likewise, we have avoided abbreviations in these books; the only one used which is not in current everyday English is L1, i.e. the students' mother tongue.

Although all of the ideas in these books are presented in English, you may need to explain or even try some of them, at least initially, in the students' L1. There is nothing wrong with this: L1 can be a useful, efficient resource, especially for explaining methodology. New ideas, which may challenge the traditional methods of teaching and learning, can be very threatening to both teachers and students. So, especially with lower-level classes, you can make them less threatening by translating them. This is not wasting time in the English class, as these ideas will help the students to learn/study more efficiently and learn more English in the long term.

Using resources with children

This resource book is designed for teachers of English, working with children aged between 8 and 11. It is intended for teachers who already have some experience of primary teaching and follows on from *An Introduction to Teaching Children*, in the same series.

The principles of developing resources for primary levels

When developing these materials the following principles have been considered.

- Children learn by doing.
- Children learn better in a positive classroom atmosphere.
- Variety is motivating.
- Different children learn in different ways.
- English can be used to explore broader themes, such as cross-cultural issues, tolerance, social behaviour.
- It is important for all activities to be relevant to the target age group, both in terms of interest levels and linguistic content, but activities can be adapted to suit the needs of different pupils, also of mixed-level classes.
- The activities should be easy to set up and carry out; moreover the activities should not require expensive or complicated resources. Teachers often need access to a bank of ideas that are easy to use without complicated or protracted preparation.
- Teachers are having to meet the needs of current reforms and developments in education and therefore often need to adapt materials to their own classroom circumstances.

How to use this book

This book assumes that the primary teacher is following a published coursebook, but it accepts the fact that there are many occasions when teachers are obliged, or find it desirable, to develop additional materials for use in class. The book is divided into chapters reflecting different areas of classroom activity, e.g. games, topic work, stories. Each chapter contains ideas that will help guide you in the development and expansion of your own resources and suggests ways of broadening classroom activity.

Each chapter contains basic ideas that you can adapt to reflect the content of the coursebook you are using. It is likely that you will use the coursebook as a starting point, but then wish to supplement it with different activities. Language guidance and activity procedures are given, but they are not prescriptive.

You can choose whether you want to use the ideas on a regular basis or whether you would like to choose just a few to develop with your class throughout the year.

Each chapter contains a set of activities which have been structured to reflect current methodological approaches as well as the interests and abilities of the age group.

To ensure that the activities will be of maximum benefit and interest to your class, the organisation of the materials has been designed to allow you maximum flexibility: you can use each activity in its entirety or choose to do as many of the stages as you want.

None of the activities requires you to use unusual or expensive resources. All the processes are things that the children will be capable of doing. They are easy to manage in the classroom and can be done with large or small classes.

In order to find an activity in the book, you can either turn to the section containing, e.g. songs, and select a song, or you can use the index to select an activity based on a particular lexical field or structure.

Features of this book

Each chapter begins with a brief introduction to the activity type: reasons for using this type of activity in the classroom, how it benefits both individual pupils and the class as a whole in ways other than purely linguistic.

At the beginning of each chapter, or in some cases each activity, the pedagogical and attitudinal aims and benefits of the activity type are given. Target language and ideas for basic adaptation or extension lexis are also given here.

Most activities are divided into several sections: basic procedure or presentation followed by ideas for further exploitation or practice. You can choose to follow as many activities within each section as you want. You can also choose to do the activities in any order you want, within each section.

Within the activity notes you will find ideas intended for older children only. These ideas give guidance on how to develop the basic activities into a more independent or complex activity. There are also ideas for higher-level children. You will be able to adapt the activity for a different class or for different ability levels in the same class. You will also find homework options and ideas for evaluation referred to within the different sections of the book.

As you go through this book you will find that there are tasks set up for the teacher to do. These are designed to help you focus on the types of issues, both pedagogic and organisational, that are of relevance to the activity areas.

Each chapter has related photocopiable pages that you can use with specific activities. These are found at the back of the book. Remember: always make sure that you have a few extra copies, for children who may want to 'start again'. When you use the photocopies, make sure that the children have scissors and pencils.

Writing in a foreign language

As this book spans the age range 8–11, the issue of whether or not to expect the children to write in English becomes pertinent. Different schools/teachers take different views on this subject. Most of the activities in the book require little or no writing by the children. Often, writing stages are suggested for older students or higher-level students, who are more able to cope with writing in a foreign language. In a few cases the activity requires students to write or to copy.

Use of L1 in the class

Try to identify the times you use L1 (the children's own language), and do not get into the habit of always using it just because it's quicker. Over-using L1 can result in English becoming a purely academic exercise, where the relevance and communicative nature of the language is lost. However, there are occasions when it is sometimes quicker and more effective to explain the aim of an activity or certain procedures in L1.

For further ideas and guidance on the use of L1 see *Helping Students to Speak*, in the same series.

Use of English for classroom instructions

The following list contains basic classroom language that we suggest you use in conjunction with the activities contained in this book. Try to use the same instructions for the same type of task. Try to always say these things in English. The children will soon get to understand their meaning and will often use these phrases themselves. Using English like this takes the language beyond the limitations of the coursebook and helps to give it an immediate and genuine relevance.

Suggested classroom language

Teacher language	Teacher/pupil language
Are you ready?	*Look, please.*
Watch carefully.	*Look at …, please.*
Listen carefully.	*Say … (a number, letter, animal, etc.).*
Get out your … (pencils, scissors, etc.).	*It's your turn.*
Stand up, everybody.	*Yes, that's right.*
Sit down, everybody.	*Go to …*
Draw the …	*Choose a …*
Colour the …	*What's missing?*
Cut out the …	*Thank you.*
Write …	*Yes.*
Copy me.	*No.*
Listen, please.	
Listen and repeat, please.	
Stop.	
Stand still.	
Don't move.	
Close your eyes.	
Work in groups.	
Work in pairs.	
Put your hands up.	
Put your hands down.	
Try again.	
Start again.	
Be quiet, please.	

Chapters of the book

Chapters 1 and 2: Games

The games contained in these chapters are divided into two types: short, ten-minute 'filler' games, and slightly longer-lasting action games. They are not intended as whole lesson plans. The games all start with a version of how to play with the whole class. Where applicable, there are ideas on how to use the game with pairs and smaller groups. They can be used to consolidate lesson activities; to provide a change in focus and pace from coursebook activities; to provide revision and consolidation practice; to give the children something enjoyable and motivating to do at the end of a lesson, when they might otherwise be getting tired.

Chapter 3: Action rhymes, songs and chants

The rhymes and songs included here consist of some which can be done in the classroom, and others which require extra space for the children to move about and a place where they can make a bit of noise without disturbing other classes. Each of the activities contained in this chapter is presented as a complete lesson plan, designed to last about 50 minutes. You can choose whether you want to follow all the stages or whether you want to choose a few to do. The rhymes and chants can also be adapted to be used as songs. The easiest way to do this is to choose a song that the children are already familiar with (this could be from your coursebook or a traditional song or rhyme). Where songs have been included and you don't know the tune, you can either try to fit the song to a tune you or the children know, or treat it as a chant. In all cases the stressed syllables have been given (') to help you with the rhythm.

Chapter 4: Things to make and use throughout the school year

This chapter is intended to present a range of ideas which will allow you to build up inexpensive and attractive resources. Each of the activities contained in this chapter is something for you to prepare and to then use with your class. Notes are given on how to make and organise these resources and then on how to use them in class. They are all things which will enhance activity in the classroom, helping to broaden English activity from being purely coursebook-driven. You can decide how many of these activities you want to do and when. You might like to do one a term, or to introduce them when they reflect a topic that is being covered in the coursebook.

Chapter 5: Simple topic work

There are two topic extension ideas in this book. They are both designed to provide maximum flexibility in terms of timing, and can be used for anything between one and six lessons. The topics have been organised in such a way that you can apply the principles and procedures to topics of your own choice.

Chapter 6: Class surveys

Survey activities provide an enjoyable and easy way to personalise English, giving the language a genuine communicative value. Surveys also enable you to build class identity and a sense of co-operation. Many coursebooks include survey ideas, but here we provide a flexible pattern of activities that you can use to reflect any topic or language area. Each of the survey activities is presented as a complete lesson plan, designed to last about 50 minutes.

Chapter 7: Story activities

One of the most enjoyable and effective ways of teaching children a foreign language is through story exploitation. Children love stories and therefore are intrinsically motivated. New language is presented in context and is often repeated through the story, allowing the children to learn it as they enjoy the story. The two stories in this chapter are well-known children's stories with elements of repetitive language. The chapter presents a series of activities to exploit the stories, and these can be adapted to accompany other stories that you might want to use with the children.

10-minute games

"Why do games work well?"

Genuine games always have an aim and purpose. They can provide a meaningful context for activity. Games are fun and enjoyment helps to develop both a positive classroom atmosphere and a more effective learning environment. Games tend to have a repetitive and cumulative nature and are therefore effective for consolidating and reinforcing language structures and lexis. They help the children to develop linguistically.

Other benefits of games are as follows.

- They reflect the children's interest level and usual behaviour.
- They help the children's cognitive development.
- They help the children to explore social behaviour and feelings.
- They help children identify with their peer group.
- They help to provide variety in the language learning approach.
- They can be effectively used to evaluate the class's performance, in a non-threatening way.

"What are the criteria for choosing games?"

- The games should have linguistic relevance.
- They should have an aim and a purpose.
- All the children should be able to participate.
- The games should be easy and quick to set up and carry out.
- They should be fun for the children.

"Is it possible to use games for evaluation?"

Games can be used to help evaluate both your class as a group and an individual child's linguistic performance. You will soon see how easily and quickly the children play the game.

"What are the special benefits of 10-minute games?"

As the name implies, these games don't take up too much class time. They should be quick to set up and quick to play. Never let them continue too long. They can be used as a fun way to start a lesson or as a way to fill in the last few minutes of a lesson if students have completed other tasks. You can also use some of them to keep early finishers busy while the rest of the class completes a task. They are a useful and fun way to revise FOCUS LEXIS or STRUCTURES. If the children are having difficulties with a particular language point, you can go over the relevant coursebook exercises again with them and then play a 10-minute game to give them extra practice.

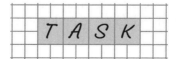

Look at the games in this chapter and tick the ones you are already familiar with. Then think about how you might be able to use the ones you don't already know.

1 Chain games

Aims of the game

The following chain games are good for consolidating syntax patterns, lexical sets and vocabulary. It is easy to adapt the games to use alphabet and number prompts.

Playing the game

1 Basic procedures

- Show the children how to play the game using animal lexis. Choose two confident children to help you.
- Say *I've got a dog.* Ask Child A to repeat what you said and to say another animal, e.g. *I've got a dog and a cat.*
- Ask Child B to repeat what Child A said, and to add another animal, *I've got a dog, a cat and a mouse.*
- Check that the pupils have understood what they have to do, then play the game with the whole class. See how many words the children can remember. When the chain breaks down, because somebody cannot remember the sequence, get the child (or the whole class), to count to twenty and then start again.

Adapting for higher levels

Higher-level pupils might like to make more complex sentences, adding adjectives, e.g. *I've got a small dog. I've got a small dog and a big cat.*

2 Extending the game: number prompts

This game can easily be adapted to use number prompts with lexical sets.

- Ask Child A to start the game saying *I've got one shoe.*
- Ask Child B to repeat what Child A said and to say another item of clothing, e.g. *I've got one shoe and two jumpers.*
- Ask Child C to repeat what Child B said, and to add another item of clothing, e.g. *I've got one shoe, two jumpers and three hats,* etc.

Adapting for higher levels

Higher levels might like to play the game using more than one lexical set at a time, for example mixing family members and transport words.

3 Extending the game: alphabet chains

Another way to play this game is to make chains using each letter of the alphabet to start each word.

- Child A would start with the letter A, saying *I've got an apple.* Child B would then say *I've got an apple and a book.* Child C would say *I've got an apple, a book and a car.* If there are letters that will be difficult for the children to use, ask the whole class to suggest words that can be used.
- Alternatively, write the problem letters on the board and tell the children to miss them out. For example, it might be difficult for the children to find words beginning with the following letters: K Q V X Y Z.

4 Children playing in groups

The children can easily play this game in groups of five or six. Encourage them to help each other and to see how long they can keep the game going for.

2 What's missing?

Aims of the game

This is a game that is good for revising lexical sets and vocabulary. It can be extended to practise reading and writing skills.

Playing the game

1 Basic procedure

- Collect together between five and ten picture FLASHCARDS illustrating words that you want to revise or consolidate with the children.
- Line up the FLASHCARDS at the front of the class. Ask the children to identify each of the items. Then give them one minute to memorise the words.
- Tell the children to close their eyes. Remove one of the FLASHCARDS. Then tell the children to open their eyes and to see if they can spot which one has disappeared.
- Repeat this process until all the words have gone.

Adapting for older children

Older children might like to take the role of teacher and to lead this game.

2 Extending the game: words

You can use this game to practise reading skills.

- Play the game in the same way, but rather than using picture FLASHCARDS, write words on the board for the children to memorise. Alternatively, if your FLASHCARDS have the words written on the back of them, you can line them up as described in the basic procedures.

Adapting for higher levels

Higher-level children might like to play the game by writing down a list of missing items, rather than calling them out. Check the answers with the whole class.

3 Extending the game: realia

You can also play this game using REALIA for certain lexical sets, such as classroom objects.

- Place the objects at the front of the class, where everybody can see them, e.g. on your desk. Then play the game, removing one of the objects, and putting it in a bag.
- This game can also be played using items of clothing. Alternatively, the children can then play in pairs, using the contents of their pencil cases.

4 Numbers, letters and board drawings

For numbers and letters of the alphabet you can write them on the board and rub single items out, for the children to guess. If you are confident about drawing pictures on the board, you could play the game by drawing a set of objects and then rubbing them out.

5 Children playing in teams

Divide the class into two teams and give one set of FLASHCARDS to each team. The teams then take it in turns to guess the missing word. If you want you can award a point to each team, each time they successfully guess the missing word.

3 Buzz!

Aims of the game

This is a game that is good for revising numbers, lexical sets and letters of the alphabet. It is easy to adapt the game to use actions.

Playing the game

1 Basic procedure

You can play this game using numbers 1 to 10, 1 to 20, 1 to 50 or 1 to 100.

- Show the children how to play the game using numbers. Choose two confident children to help you. Ask Child A to start counting, and to say *1*. Ask Child B to say *2*. Ask Child C to say *3*. Then take your turn and say *Buzz!* (Or rather than saying *Buzz!*, you could say the name of your coursebook.)

- Explain to the children that they have to count, but that every fourth child has to say *Buzz!* rather than a number. The next child then continues counting from the next number, e.g. *1, 2, 3, Buzz!, 4, 5, 6, Buzz!, 7, 8*, etc.

- Then play the game with the whole class. When the children forget to say *Buzz!* get them to stand up and turn around.

Adapting for older or higher-level children

Older children or higher-level pupils might like to play the game using only odd, even or multiple numbers, e.g. Odd: *1, 3, 5, Buzz!, 7*; Even: *2, 4, 6, Buzz!, 8*; Multiples: *5, 10, 15, Buzz!, 20*. Alternatively, they can substitute *Buzz!* for numbers, e.g. *1, 2, Buzz!, 4, 5, Buzz!, 7, 8*, etc.

2 Adapting the game: lexical sets

You can also play this game using lexical sets, the first three children saying three words and the fourth child saying *Buzz!*

3 Adapting the game: alphabet

Another way to play this game is using letters of the alphabet. The first three children say *A, B, C*, and the fourth child says *Buzz!*

4 Adapting the game: actions

Play the game, but rather than saying the word *Buzz!*, get every fourth child to give the rest of the class an instruction. For example, *1, 2, 3, Stand up!, 4, 5, 6, Turn around!*, etc. The rest of the class should carry out the action.

5 Children playing in groups

The children can easily play any variation of this game in groups of five. Do not play in groups of four as the same child will always say *Buzz!*

4 Categories

Aims of the game

This is a game that is good for revising lexical sets.

Playing the game

1 Basic procedure

- Choose five categories of lexis that you would like to practise with the children and then show the children how to play the game.
- Either draw a grid on the board and ask the children to copy it into their exercise books, or give the children a photocopied grid.

Animal	Food	Family	Colour	Sport

- Give an example of what they have to do. Elicit from the class one word for each of the categories, and write them in.

Animal	Food	Family	Colour	Sport
fish	bread	mum	red	tennis

- Then give the children three minutes (or however long you think the children need) to fill in as many words as they can. Allow them to use their coursebooks or dictionaries to help.
- Let the children compare their answers with a friend, and fill in any gaps they may have. Check the answers with the whole class and see how many words they found for each category.

Adapting for older children

Older children might like to play this game in teams. Divide the class into pairs or teams of four. Give each team a grid to complete.

Adapting for higher levels

Higher-level pupils might like to play the game using sequential letters of the alphabet or even words with 2, 3, 4, etc. letters in them. Let the children use plural forms, but if you play the game this way, tell the children that not all letters will have appropriate words.

Letter	2	3	4	5
A	an	and	arms	apple
B	by	but	bike	buses
C	–	can	can't	cooks

5 The 'Pen' game

Aims of the game

This is a writing game that is good for revising vocabulary items and for recognition of words outside the confines of a lexical set.

Playing the game

1 Basic procedure

- Show the children how to play the game. Write a word on the board, e.g. *pen*. Then elicit a word beginning with each of the letters from the class. Write the words next to each letter.

> P e n c i l
> E l e p h a n t
> N o s e

- Ask the children to take a piece of paper or their exercise books. Dictate words to them, or write words on the board for the children to copy.
- Then let the children work in pairs to see how many of the word puzzles they can complete. Check the answers with the whole class and see how many words the children thought of.
- If you've already covered plurals, you might like to play the game using only plural words, e.g. P – pencils, E – elephants, N – noses.

2 Extending the game: flashcards

Hold up a FLASHCARD and ask the children to write the word, e.g. *bus*. Then let them play the game in pairs as before.

3 Extending the game: making sentences

Once the pairs have completed each word puzzle they might like to try to make sentences using each word, e.g. *I've got lots of pencils. I like elephants.*

4 Children playing in groups

The children can easily play this game in pairs or groups of four.

5 Adapting the game: word steps

This game can easily be adapted: rather than asking the children to use each letter in a word, ask them to make steps using the last letter of each word. See how many steps the children can make, without repeating a word, e.g.

> Pen
> 1 nose
> 2   elephant
> 3   tree
> 4   ear

6 Homework option

You could easily adapt this game to include a homework activity by giving the children one or two base words and asking them to play the game at home.

6 Consequences

Aims of the game

This is a traditional game that is good for writing skills and sequencing. It is easy to adapt the game to use picture consequences.

Playing the game

1 Basic procedure

- Give each child a blank piece of paper (half an A4 sheet cut vertically is ideal) and explain how to play the game. The four basic steps are as follows:
  1 They write something, according to the questions you give them.
  2 They fold their paper over, so that nobody can see what they've written.
  3 They give the paper to the person sitting next to them.
  4 They repeat steps 1 to 3 with a new question.
- Show the children how they must fold the paper after they have written each section.
- Guide the game by asking the children to think of an imaginary character and then asking them questions. Ask:

  What's your name?
  How old are you?
  How many eyes have you got?
  How many legs have you got?
  What colour are you?
  Who is your best friend?

- When everybody has finished, tell them to pass the paper on one more time and then let the children unravel their consequence sheet and read the description. You can ask the children to tell each other or the class about their character.

  My name's …
  I'm 34.
  I've got 26 eyes.
  I've got 13 legs.
  I'm green and pink.
  My best friend is …

- Finally, you can then ask the children to write a description of their character and to draw a picture. Put the sentences the children will need to use on the board for them to copy.

2 Adapting the game: picture consequences

Prepare the paper as before. Ask the children to draw a part of the body on each section of the paper. You will need to tell the children which sections of the body to concentrate on: head and neck, body and arms, legs, feet. The children will need to fold the paper leaving guide lines for the next child to follow. The children can then give their character a name and write about it.

7 Cross the road

Aims of the game

This is a quiz comprehension game. You will need to prepare the questions before using this activity in class.

Playing the game

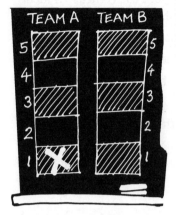

1 Basic procedure

- Draw two zebra crossings on the board.
- Divide the class into two teams. Ask each team a question in turn. If they answer correctly, they advance one stripe across the zebra crossing. (Draw a cross on the crossing.) The first team to cross the road is the winner.
- Use the coursebook and FLASHCARDS to make your questions. Remember to give each team matching questions. For example, if you ask Team A to identify a food FLASHCARD, ask Team B to identify another food FLASHCARD.
- If your class is arranged in rows of desks you could ask all the children in the front row to answer a question, then all the children in the second row to answer the next question, etc.
- If you do not want this to be a competitive game, play the game with the whole class, using one longer zebra crossing.

2 Homework option

Ask the children to think of a question and write it down for the next game.

8 Anagrams

Aims of the game

This is word game that helps to consolidate letter order. It can easily be adapted to practise sentence formation.

Playing the game

1 Word anagrams

- Write the letters of a word on the board. Write them in random order, e.g. for *ruler* write *e r r l u*. Show the children how to solve the puzzle.
- Repeat the process with more words that you want the children to practise. The children write each of the words on a piece of paper or in their books.
- Check the answers with the whole class.

Adapting for higher levels

Higher-level children might like to play this game in pairs. Each child can prepare anagram words which they then give to the other child to solve.

2 Sentence anagrams

- Write the words of a sentence on the board in random order. Use structures that reflect the language you are covering in the coursebook, e.g. *book she's reading a* = *She's reading a book*.
- Show the children how to decipher the sentences. Remind them about capital letters and full stops.

9 Flashcard matching

Aims of the game

This is a game which practises word recognition skills.

Playing the game

1 Basic procedure: non-competitive game

- Place a set of picture FLASHCARDS at the front of the class. Hold each one up and ask the class to identify it.
- Write the words for each FLASHCARD on the board. Read them with the class.
- Ask a child, or a pair of children to come to the front. Say a word and encourage the children to pick up the FLASHCARD. Then they should go to the board and circle the corresponding word.
- Repeat this process until all the words have been covered.

2 Competitive game

To make this into a competitive game, divide the class into two teams. Children from the teams then take it in turns to come and match the pictures and words.

3 Word matching

Rather than using picture FLASHCARDS and words written on the board, you might like to try this variation: ask the children to identify words written on pieces of paper and then to find the corresponding word written on the board.

10 Flashcard categorisation

Aims of the game

This game practises vocabulary recognition and categorisation skills.

Playing the game

1 Basic procedure: non-competitive game

- Place three sets of FLASHCARDS (jumbled) at the front of the class. Divide the board into three and write the category of each section at the top.
- Ask pairs of children to come to the front of the class. Say a word from one of the sets. The children should pick up the picture FLASHCARD and then stick it under the appropriate category on the board. Use BLU-TACK for this, so that you do not spoil the FLASHCARDS.

2 Extending the game: writing practice

This game can be extended to writing practice by asking the children to identify a picture card, which they stick on the board in the appropriate category and then asking them to write the word underneath.

Look back at the games in this chapter. How many of them could be played with the whole class, how many in smaller groups, and how many could be used as extra activities for fast finishers? Mark the different activities Whole class, Groups, Fast Finishers. (Check your answers with the Key on PAGE 95.)

Action games

"Why do games work well and what are the criteria for choosing them?"

Chapter 1 on 10-minute games gives a general introduction into why games work well in the language classroom, what the criteria are for choosing games, and how games can be used in evaluating your students. ◆ SEE 10-MINUTE GAMES PAGE 9

"What are 'action' games?"

As the name implies, action games require the pupils to move about and they may make quite a lot of noise when playing them. It is therefore recommended that you find a suitable place to play them – perhaps the playground or the school hall or gym. Alternatively, find a classroom where you can move the furniture to one side, and where you know that any noise will not disturb other classes nearby. These games will need more time than the games in Chapter 1.

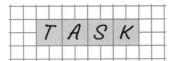
T A S K

Think of as many reasons as you can for using action games with primary school children.

1 What's the time, Mr Wolf?

Aims of the game

This is a traditional game that is useful for practising or revising telling the time (numbers 1 to 12, and *o'clock*) and the question *What's the time?* It is useful to extend the game to include *quarter past*, *half past*, and *quarter to*. It is simple to play with beginners, but this game must be played in the playground or hall because of the noise. The game works best with a maximum of ten players so divide larger classes into groups.

Playing the game

1 Basic procedure

● Find a space in the playground and show the children how to play the game. Choose one child to be Mr Wolf. He/she must stand against a wall, facing the wall. Show them how to stand so that they cannot see the other children. Choose six to ten children to play the game. They must stand in a line about ten metres behind Mr Wolf. The remainder of the class sits on the ground to watch.

● First, say to the class *What's the time, Mr Wolf?* and ask the children to repeat it. Tell Mr Wolf to say *It's two o'clock!* and ask the class to repeat the time.

● Now, tell the players to start walking slowly towards Mr Wolf and to chorus *What's the time, Mr Wolf?*

● Tell Mr Wolf to say *It's two o'clock!* and to turn round quickly. The players must stop and stand as still as possible, like statues. If Mr Wolf sees anyone moving, that player must go back to the start.

- Mr Wolf then turns back to the wall and the players start walking forward again, and ask *What's the time, Mr Wolf?* again. Each time Mr Wolf must say a different time.
- At any point in the game Mr Wolf can answer *It's dinner time*, then turn round and run to catch one of the players. If he catches someone they become Mr Wolf.
- The game starts again and continues until all the children have had a go.
- With big classes choose another group to play the game while the others watch or have two groups playing the game at the same time.

2 Extending the game: different times, different meals

- Tell Mr Wolf to say a time with *half past* or *quarter past* or *quarter to the hour.*
- Tell Mr Wolf to change the meals as well, e.g. *It's teatime/breakfast time/supper time.*

3 Extending the game: coursebook guessing game

- This could be done back in the classroom. Choose a page in the coursebook which shows the topic of time in detail.
- Ask the class to divide into pairs, A and B. Child A looks at the page and chooses a time on the clock. B tries to guess what time A is thinking of and asks *What's the time, Mr Wolf? Is it 7 o'clock?* They can have five guesses.
- When they guess correctly or if they fail to guess after five goes, change over and repeat the activity.

2 Postman

Aims of the game

This is a traditional game that is useful for learning the names of countries or towns. You can extend the activity to writing postcards or letters, after the game. You play it with the whole class together in the hall, gym or playground.

Lexis: *hop, skip, crawl, run;* names of towns and countries; *letter, card, parcel.*

Teacher preparation

Write the names of countries or towns which are known to the children on strips of paper so that there are enough to give one place to each child.

Equipment needed: one scarf for a blindfold, strips of paper for names.

Playing the game

1 Basic procedure

- Show the children how to play the game. Start by asking the children to sit in a circle on the floor. Ask one child to be the person in the middle. This child stands in the middle and is blindfolded.
- Give every child the name of a country or town. Keep a list of these names for yourself.
- Explain that you are going to post things from one place to another, e.g. *I'm sending a letter from London to Madrid.* Tell the children who have these place names to cross to the other side of the circle (i.e. to change places) without being caught by the child in the middle.

- Write these instructions on the board or on a large piece of card if you're going to play this outside. Students must cross the circle in the following ways:

    … for a letter they hop.
    … for an express letter they run.
    … for a postcard they crawl.
    … for a parcel they skip.

    As they cross the circle they must say *I am going to France/Madrid,* etc.

- When they are caught, they change places with the child in the middle.

Note: Ensure that you supervise this game carefully to minimise the risks of overexcitement and accidents.

2 Adapting the game: Who's wearing …?

- This is played sitting on a circle of chairs. Explain to the children that they can cross the circle when the child in the centre says *Who's wearing the colour …?* It is not necessary to have a blindfold.

- They must cross the circle as fast as possible as the teacher takes away one chair each time. The child who does not have a seat is out.

- It is best to stop the game after five or six colours and change the child in the centre of the circle. Change the focus to who's wearing certain items of clothing, e.g. trousers, jumpers, dresses, types of shoes (sandals, trainers, lace-ups, shoes with straps, etc.) The children change places when the one in the middle says *Who's wearing …?*

3 The circus

Aims of the game

This is a traditional game which is useful to teach or revise the vocabulary of animals and the noises they make. It can be used as an extension to an animal story or a coursebook topic on animals. You play with the whole class together, or divided into groups if your class has more than about 15 pupils. You will need to be in the hall, gym or playground.

Lexis: *horse, elephant, tiger, lion, snake, monkey, parrot, ringmaster*; animal noises; instruction: *Make the noise like …*; question: *What noise does a … make?*

Extension lexis: *roar, growl, hiss, chatter, squawk, moo, bleat, cluck, crow, quack.*

Equipment needed: a scarf for a blindfold.

Playing the game

1 Basic procedure

- Show the children how to play the game. Write the names of the circus animals on the board or a large piece of paper, and if necessary for your class, go through/revise the names and noises that the animals make.

- Ask the class to stand in a circle. Choose one child to be the ringmaster and to stand in the middle of the circle, blindfolded.

- The children hold hands and skip around the ringmaster until the ringmaster shouts *Stop!*

- The ringmaster then points to one of the children and says *What noise does a … make?*, naming whichever circus animal he/she chooses. The other child can repeat the noise three times and say *It makes a … noise.*
- The ringmaster must guess who is making the noise.
- If the ringmaster guesses correctly, the two children change over. If he/she does not guess correctly, continue the game.

2 Extending the game: using your coursebook

- Find the page in your coursebook which has a picture of circus or farm animals.
- Point to, e.g. a horse; ask the class *What noise does a horse make?*
- Reply *A horse neighs.* Ask the class to repeat this and make the noise.
- Point to an elephant and ask the class *What noise does an elephant make?*
- Reply *An elephant trumpets.* Ask the class to repeat this and make the noise.
- Continue the exercise, pointing to each animal and making the noise: *a lion roars   a tiger growls   a snake hisses   a monkey chatters   a parrot squawks*
- The exercise can be extended to farm animals: *a cow moos   a sheep bleats a chicken/hen clucks   a cockerel crows   a duck quacks*
- If you prefer, you could do this activity before playing the game. When the ringmaster asks, e.g. *What noise does a lion make?* The child can reply *A lion roars* and can then make the noise.

4 The 'Yes/No' game

Aims of the game

This is a game that is useful for revising any vocabulary areas that have been learned. It is easily adapted as an activity at the end of a lesson.

Teacher preparation

Write a list of general questions which require the answer *Yes* or *No*, e.g. *Is Rome the capital of England? Is it raining today?* etc. or personal questions, e.g. *Do you like sweets?*

Playing the game

1 Basic procedure

- Draw a line down the middle of a space in the classroom or playground or stretch a string along the floor.
- Ask the children to stand on one side of the line or string. Tell them *This side is No, the other side is Yes.*
- Ask the children *Has a horse got four legs?* Tell the children, if the answer is *Yes*, they must jump to the Yes side of the line or string.
- Ask the children *Is it raining today?* Wait for a reply. Tell them to either jump or stay on the Yes side.

Adapting for higher levels

Ask the children to make up their own questions. Then let the children take turns to read their questions to the rest of the class.

5 Cat and mouse

Aims of the game

This is a simple game for the whole class that is useful for teaching directions, e.g. *turn right, turn left*. It is a game that can be extended for larger classes to include other animals.

Lexis: *change, turn left, turn right; start, ready, steady, go.*

Playing the game

1 Basic procedure

- Show the children how to play the game. Find a large space in the hall, gym or in the playground as the children need space to run around. Choose two children to be the cat and the mouse and tell the rest of the class to make three or four rows; they must spread out, face the same way and hold hands down the rows. These children form a sort of maze.

- Say *Ready, steady, go!* to start the game. The mouse runs between the rows and the cat then chases the mouse.

- Call out a change of direction: *Change, turn right.* The children whose arms are making the walls of the maze all drop hands and change direction. They turn to their right and hold hands across the rows. Then say *Change, turn left.*

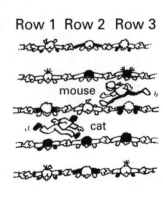

- When the mouse is caught that game ends. Choose a new cat and mouse and play again. To make the cat's task harder, give two children the role of mouse.

2 Extending the game: other animals

For variety, choose other animals, e.g. a fox and a chicken, a lion and a rabbit, etc.

T A S K

Go through the five action games in this chapter. Which ones are appropriate for your situation in terms of a) language and b) physical activity? Choose one of the games and try it with your class.

Action rhymes, songs and chants

"Why use action rhymes, songs and chants with your class?"

These are a flexible resource for the language teacher and have a number of benefits.

- They make learning more memorable.
- They are an excellent way of practising rhythm and stress.
- Children learn songs and rhymes easily and quickly. They enjoy them and children of all language abilities can join in, which helps build confidence.
- Most songs and rhymes are made of prefabricated phrases with new words added between the set phrases.
- Songs and rhymes introduce children naturally and effectively to the sounds of English as well as stress and intonation.
- They are a way of giving children a complete text with meaning from the first lesson.
- If songs and rhymes are carefully selected and slotted into your teaching programme they can be used to introduce or practise new language, e.g. *has got* or animals in song 1 or numbers in rhyme 2 below.

Each of the activities contained in this chapter is presented as a complete lesson plan, designed to last about 50 minutes.

1 Song: The farmer's in his den

Aims of the song

This is an adaptation of a traditional song that is good for revising animal lexis. It is easy to extend the animal lexis or to adapt to other lexical areas. This song can be used in conjunction with masks in CHAPTER 5, PAGE 53.

Extension lexis: any other animals.

Adaptation lexis: family members, clothes, food and transport.

Materials needed: coursebook, animal FLASHCARDS, music, paper, pens, pencils, large sheets of paper for posters.

The song

Chorus
The 'farmer's in his 'den.
The 'farmer's in his 'den.
'E 'I 'O 'U
The 'farmer's in his 'den.

1st verse
The 'farmer's got a 'dog.
The 'farmer's got a 'dog.
'E 'I 'O 'U
The 'farmer's got a 'dog.

Other verses: The 'farmer's got a 'cat/'hen/'pig/'horse/'cow.

Preparation

1 Basic procedure

Use a page from your coursebook to practise recognition of animal lexis. Ask the children to open their books and point to the animals as you say them. Then say the animals that the children can see on the page, leaving one of them out. The children should tell you which one is missing.

Adapting for higher levels

For higher-level children you could to extend this to a writing activity. Repeat the above procedure, but rather than getting the children to call out the missing animal, get them to write it down on a piece of paper. Then check all the answers with the whole class.

2 Guessing game

Using a page from your coursebook or a set of animal FLASHCARDS, play a simple game with the class.

- Describe an animal and see if the class can guess which animal you are referring to. Describe its body, its colour and its size. Depending on the context of the page or FLASHCARD, you could also describe where it is or what it's doing. When the children guess the animal they can all mime it.

Adapting for older or higher-level children

Older children or higher-level students could get into pairs or groups and play this game themselves. Each child should take it in turns to describe an animal, while the other children have to guess.

3 Class activity: animal statues

- Play some music. Ask the children to stand up and move around the class, playground or gym, pretending to be a farmer.
- When the music stops the children should stand still, like statues.
- Say an animal and get the children to mime it. They could also make the noise of the animal. When you put the music on again, they should stop miming the animal and pretend to be the farmer again.

Presentation

1 Basic procedure

- Draw a simple picture of a stick man on the board, and tell the children that this is the farmer. Then draw a house and say that this is his house or 'den'.
- Take a FLASHCARD, or draw a picture, of each animal in the song. Tell the children that *The farmer's got a …* and stick the picture up on the board.
- Ask the children to tell you what animals the farmer has got. Say one of the animals and ask the children to make the noise of the animal.
- If you want to use this as a song, ask the children to hum the tune before you ask them to sing the words to the song. Sing two lines from the song and get the children to repeat after you. Gradually build up the song, until the children can sing it all.

Adapting for higher levels

Higher-level students might like to choose the farm animals for themselves. Elicit a set of animals from the class and use these to sing the song.

Practice

1 Exploiting the song: roleplay

- Ask the class to sing the song and to act it out.
- Divide the class into six groups (one group for each animal mentioned in the song). Then choose a child to pretend to be the farmer.
- The child who is pretending to be the farmer should walk around the class. As the children sing the song, they should pretend to be their assigned animal. As each animal is mentioned in the song, the children should form a line and follow the farmer.

2 Class activity: make a poster

- Ask the children to choose one of the animals from the song, then give each child a piece of paper and ask them to draw the animal they have chosen.
- The children should then cut out their animal pictures and stick them on to a large sheet of paper, making a farm poster. In large classes you could split the class into several groups so that the children can make three or four posters. The children can also draw speech bubbles, containing the noises the animals make.

Adapting for higher levels

You can extend this to a simple writing exercise. The children could write labels for the animals or write simple descriptions about the poster, e.g. *There are/The farmer's got six cows*, etc.

3 Song adaptation: other lexical areas

You could use any of these ideas to present and practise vocabulary from other lexical groups, e.g. family lexis: *The farmer's got a son/daughter/wife/granny*, etc.; transport lexis: *The farmer's got a car/tractor/bike/plane*, etc.

4 Homework option

Get the children to draw one of the animals and to write *The farmer's got a …* Collect these pictures together and make a class display.

2 Rhyme: One potato, two potatoes

Aims of the rhyme

This is a traditional rhyme that British children use to decide who is going to lead a game or carry out a specific task. It is an activity that has a genuine relevance and application to children's lives and experience.

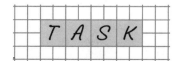

Think of a similar rhyme that the children in your class might use in L1 as this will help you to present the rhyme to the children.

The rhyme

'One po'tato, 'two po'tatoes, 'three po'tatoes, 'four.
'Five po'tatoes, 'six po'tatoes, 'seven po'tatoes, 'more.

Presentation

1 Basic procedure

- Explain to the children that they are all going to learn a rhyme that British children say. Then tell them how it is used and why. ◆ SEE *AIMS OF THE RHYME ABOVE*.

- Demonstrate how to say the rhyme. Ask four children to come to the front of the class. Ask the children to close their fingers around their thumbs and to hold out their fists. Their fists are the 'potatoes'.

- Say the rhyme. Go round the group in order, touching one fist each time you count *One (potato), two (potatoes), three (potatoes)*, etc.

- When you say *more* the child whose fist you have just touched should put that hand behind their back.

- Repeat this process until just one child is left with one fist held out. This is the child who is designated as leader for any subsequent game.

Practice

1 Saying the rhyme in pairs

- Ask the children to work in pairs. Child A in each pair should hold up their fingers. Child B is going to do the counting.

- Say the rhyme, and encourage the children to count with you. As you count Child B should touch Child A's fingers. When you say *more* Child A should hold down the finger that was the last to be counted.

- Remind the children that as they count again, they must not include the finger that was just touched when you said *more*.

- See if everybody has finished with the same finger. Swap roles and repeat.

2 Saying the rhyme in groups

Divide the class into groups of five. Four children hold out their fists and one child counts. Say the chant as a whole class, with the different groups acting it out. Then let the children say the rhyme in their individual groups.

3 Class activity: colour the rhyme

- Give each child a copy of PHOTOCOPIABLE PAGE 1.
- Use colours that the children need extra practice with and tell the children to colour in the potatoes. Say *Potato number 1 is green, potato number 2 is red*, etc.
- When the children have coloured in their chant picture, check the colours by asking *What colour's potato number 5?* etc. Then say the rhyme together, pointing at the potatoes in sequence. The children put a small cross in the corner of each potato picture that coincides with the word *more*.
- Finally see if the children can tell you which potato is left at the end. They should all have the same answer.

4 Exploiting the rhyme and photocopies: colour bingo

You could use the pages the children have coloured to play colour bingo.

- Ask the children to choose three colours and to draw a circle around those potatoes. Then say the colours in random order, e.g. *brown potato, green potato*, etc.
- As the children hear the colours they **haven't** circled, they should draw a circle around the corresponding potato. As soon as a child has a circle round all his/her potatoes, he/she should shout *Bingo!*

5 Homework option

Ask the children to use the rhyme when they want to decide who is the leader in a playground game. You can set this as 'homework'.

3 Rhyme or song: Hickory dickory dock

Aims of the rhyme

This is an adaptation of a traditional rhyme said by British children. The language has been adapted here so that the children can say the rhyme using the present tense. It can easily be adapted to practise telling the time.

Materials needed: coursebook or FLASHCARDS of numbers 1 to 12; one copy for each child of PHOTOCOPIABLE PAGE 2; coloured pencils, scissors and glue.

The rhyme/song

'Hickory, 'dickory, 'dock.
The 'mouse runs 'up the 'clock.
The 'clock says 'one.
The 'mouse runs 'down.
'Hickory, 'dickory, 'dock.

Preparation

1 Basic procedure

Use a page from your coursebook or a set of number FLASHCARDS to practise recognition of numbers 1 to 12. Ask the children to look at the coursebook page or the FLASHCARDS. Say a number (1 to 11), and ask the children to tell you what comes next. Then ask the children to count around the class.

2 Game: Think of a number

Play a simple game with the children. Explain that you are going to think of a number from 1 to 12, and that the children have to guess which number it is. Think of a number, e.g. 7. Ask the children to say a number; if the number is lower than 7, say *higher*. If the number is higher than 7, say *lower*. When the children guess the number say *Yes, that's right.* The children can then play the game in pairs or groups.

Adapting the game for higher levels

With higher-level pupils you could play the game using odd or even numbers, or to count up to 20 or 50.

3 Class activity: mouse mime

You'll need plenty of room for this activity, so you might consider doing it in the hall, gym or even the playground. Invite the class to pretend to be mice and to carry out the actions you say. Say *Run, run, little mice. Jump, jump, little mice,* etc. A confident child might then like to give the rest of the class instructions.

4 Class activity: up and down

Encourage the class to focus on the words *up* and *down*. Say *Up, up, up.* And get the children to stretch up as high as they can. Then say *Down, down, down.* And get the children to crouch down as low as they can.

Presentation

1 Saying the words

Ask the class to be a clock, and to rhythmically make a ticking sound. Say the rhyme to the class with the children making the ticking sound. Draw the rhyme on the board.

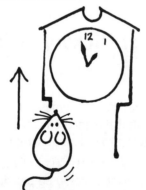

Hickory, dickory, dock.
The mouse runs up the clock.

The clock says one.

The mouse
runs down.
Hickory, dickory, dock.

- Ask the children to tell you what they think is happening in the rhyme. Then encourage the children to repeat the rhyme one line at a time.

Practice

1 Exploiting the rhyme

Divide the class into two groups. Encourage the first group to chant rhythmically *Tick tock, tick tock,* and the second group to say the rhyme. Swap roles and repeat. The children might like to record their performance onto a blank cassette.

2 Rhyme extension: telling the time

To practise telling the time, substitute the line *The clock says one* with other times. If you like, get the children to make the noise of the clock striking.

3 Rhyme adaptation: animals

Ask the children to think of some more small animals and insects. Use these to adapt the line *The mouse runs up the clock.*

4 Rhyme model: making a clock

Ask the children to make a clock in the following way.

- Give one copy of PHOTOCOPIABLE PAGE 2 to each child in the class.
- Ask the children to cut out the picture of the clock and the mouse 'strip'.
- Ask the children to think of a time for their clock and to draw it on the clock face. Make sure that the children remember to draw the big hand for *o'clock* and the small hand for the hour.
- Now ask the children to colour in their mouse.
- Then get the children to move around the class and to find other children who have drawn the same time as they have. These children should then form groups.
- Invite each group to pick up their mouse and to say the rhyme at the front of the class. They should follow the words in the rhyme moving their mouse up and down the clock by moving the mouse strip through the cut in the clock.

5 Homework option

Ask the children to draw a picture of the rhyme, choosing any time they want.

4 Chant: The wheels on the bus

Aims of the chant

This is a traditional action chant that is good for revising actions, sounds and prepositions and to introduce topics on going to town or transport. It doesn't require very much space.

Basic lexis/structures: *Where is the/are the …? It's/They're …*

Extension lexis: other items and activities on a bus.

Note: In Britain it's common to see double-decker buses as described in the rhyme, i.e. buses with an 'upstairs'. The most famous are the red ones in London, but double-deckers are found all over the country in a variety of colours.

The chant

The 'wheels on the 'bus go 'round and 'round,
'round and 'round, 'round and 'round
The 'wheels on the 'bus go 'round and 'round,
'All day 'long
The 'wipers on the 'bus go 'swish, 'swish, 'swish,
'All day 'long
The 'horn on the 'bus goes 'toot, 'toot, 'toot,
'All day 'long
The 'people on the 'bus go 'up and 'down,
'All day 'long
The 'money on the 'bus goes 'clink, 'clink, 'clink,
'All day 'long

} (all repeated as above)

Presentation

1 Basic procedure: pairwork using your coursebook

● Find a page in your coursebook which shows transport or going shopping in town and which includes a picture of a bus. Ask the children to work in pairs and to look at one book together. One child is A and the second child is B.

● Hold your book up to the class. Point to the bus and say *Here is the bus.* Child A then asks *Where is the bus?* and Child B points to the bus and says *Here is the bus.* Tell the children to exchange roles and repeat the question and answer.

● Point to the wheels on the bus. Say *Here are the wheels.* Repeat the sequence. Child A asks *Where are the wheels (on the bus)?* and Child B points to the wheels and replies *Here are the wheels.* Tell the children to exchange roles again and repeat the question and answer.

Adapting for higher levels

Higher-level pupils might like to extend the ROLEPLAY and ask questions and give answers about other things in the picture. Ask the children if this bus is different from the buses they have in their towns.

2 Guessing the actions

To introduce the chant, mime the actions in the chant first. Do the actions separately, then ask the children what you are doing.

1 *The wheels on the bus go round and round.* Pretend you are the bus wheels with your arms bent at the elbows and hands held straight. Rotate the arms as if they are wheels.

2 *The wipers on the bus go swish, swish, swish.* Hold your hands straight up in front of your face and sway your hands from left to right like windscreen wipers.

3 *The horn on the bus goes toot, toot, toot.* Make a horn with your hands and fingers curled around and placed sideways over your mouth and make a tooting noise.

4 *The people on the bus go up and down.* Mime going up the stairs using the fingers of one hand as the stairs and with the other hand bending two fingers like a pair of legs to walk up and down.

5 *The money on the bus goes clink, clink, clink.* Pretend to collect the money and shake it in a bag.

Adapting for higher levels

Higher-level pupils may like to make up other actions which happen on a bus, e.g. *The people on the bus go chatter, chatter, chatter; the babies on the bus go boo hoo hoo,* etc.

3 Class activity: miming the actions

Show the children how to mime the actions (as described above). Then let them mime while you say the chant.

Practice

1 Saying the chant

If possible, copy the chant onto a separate page and photocopy it for each child. Read the chant to the children, miming the actions where necessary, then read the chant together with the children or ask the children to repeat each line with you. Finally, practise the chant with the class in groups, using one line for each group, and doing the actions at the same time. All the class repeats the last line *All day long.*

2 Exploiting the song: drawing dictation

- Draw a basic outline of a bus on the board and choose five children to come out and draw in each of the articles and people on the bus from the rhyme (wheels, windscreen wipers, horn, people, money).

Adapting for higher levels

Higher-level students can draw other items on the bus, e.g. windows, steering wheel, bus conductor, etc.

- Ask the children to copy the picture of the bus onto a piece of paper. The children can work in pairs. Child A asks *Where are the wheels (on the bus)?* Child B points to the picture and replies *Here are the wheels.* Child A asks *Where are the wipers (on the bus)?* Child B points to the picture and replies *Here are the wipers.* Continue the questions and answers for *the horn, the people* and *the money*.

3 Song extension: other items on the bus

Ask the class to tell you some other things you may see or hear on a bus journey into town, e.g. a dog, a cat, etc. Say the chant using these items and noises.

5 Chant or song: Here we go round the mulberry bush

Aims of the song

This is a traditional action song that is good for revising parts of the body, verbs and clothes. It is easy to extend the lexis for these areas and to adapt to other lexical areas.

Extension lexis: *comb our hair, polish our shoes, run to school, jump up and down, do up our buttons, eat our breakfast.*

Questions: *What do you do …? What do you do next?*

Sequencing words: *first, next, and then.*

The song

Chorus

Here we go round the 'mulberry 'bush,
The 'mulberry 'bush, the 'mulberry 'bush,
Here we go round the 'mulberry 'bush,
On a 'cold and 'frosty 'morning.

Verse 1

This is the way we 'wash our 'hands,
'Wash our 'hands, wash our 'hands,
This is the way we 'wash our 'hands,
On a 'cold and 'frosty 'morning.

Verse 2: This is the way we 'wash our 'faces, etc.
Verse 3: This is the way we 'brush our 'hair, etc.
Verse 4: This is the way we 'clean our 'teeth, etc.
Verse 5: This is the way we 'put on our 'clothes, etc.

Presentation

1 Basic procedure: using your coursebook

Use a page from your coursebook to practise what we do first thing in the morning, i.e. wash our hands and face, brush our hair, clean our teeth, put on our clothes. Set the children up to ask and answer as follows. When they have finished, they can change roles and repeat the activity.

A: *What do you do when you get up?*
B: *I put on my clothes.*
A: *What do you do next?*
B: *I wash my hands and face.*

2 Guessing game

Mime the actions for each line to the class and ask the children to tell you what you are doing, e.g. pretend to wash your face; pretend to brush your hair; pretend to put on your clothes, e.g. jacket, trousers, shoes, coat, etc.; pretend to clean your teeth. Ask the children to think of other things which they do first thing in the morning (e.g. see Extension lexis). Ask some of the children to come to the front of the class one at a time and mime their action.

3 Class activity: sequencers *first, next, and then*

- Write the list of activities on the board in this order: *put on our clothes, clean our teeth, brush our hair, wash our hands and faces.*

- Tell the children in which order you do these things in the morning. Ask the children what other things they do in the morning and add these to the list. Then ask the class *What do you do first in the morning? What do you do next in the morning? And then what do you do?*

- Divide the class into pairs, A and B. Make sure Child B has got four actions ready. Child A asks the three questions to Child B, e.g.
  A: *What do you do first in the morning?*
  B: *First I wash my hands and face.*
  A: *What do you do next in the morning?*
  B: *Next I ... . And next I ...*
  A: *And then what do you do?*
  B: *And then I ...*

Practice

1 Saying the chant

Find a space in the gym or in the playground where the children can make a large circle. Stand in the middle.

- Read Verse 1 to the class, doing the actions for each line. The children can chant the chorus after the verse. Go through the other verses with the children and let them repeat the words with you and mime each action. Repeat the chorus after each verse.

- Now all repeat the whole chant, saying the words and doing the actions together. When they chant the chorus they can skip around in a circle – 'going round the mulberry bush'. Then stop again and mime the actions when you all say each verse.

2 Exploiting the song

- Draw four boxes and write the actions under the boxes.

Wash our face and hands	Brush our hair	Clean our teeth	Put on our clothes

- Ask the class *What do you do first in the morning?* Each child must write down what they do first. Ask *What do you do second?* Repeat the questions for third and fourth and the children write down the actions. Then ask each child to come and write the numbers in the boxes in the correct order in which they do these things in the morning.

3 Chant extension

- Look back at Presentation activity 2, where the children thought of other actions which they did first thing in the morning, e.g. *clean our shoes, run to school, do up our buttons, eat our breakfast*, etc. Say the chant with these actions, miming them at the same time.
- Ask the children *What do you do before you go to bed and in what order?* Ask them to mime these actions.

Adapting for higher levels

Higher-level students can make up more involved actions and say them to the same rhyme followed by the chorus.

4 Game: Chinese Whispers on a cold and frosty morning

- Ask the children to sit on the floor in two or three circles, each with a maximum of ten children. Tell the children that you are going to pass on a chain message by whispering it in someone's ear. Begin the message with *On a cold and frosty morning I …*
- The child you whispered to now whispers the message to the child on his/her left, who whispers it in turn to the child on his/her left, etc. Tell the children that it doesn't matter if they don't totally understand what they hear, they must just whisper what they think they heard to the next child.
- When the message reaches the last child, he/she says it aloud and compares it with the original message. The fun of the game comes from hearing a totally distorted sentence at the end of the chain.

6 Rhyme or song: Incey Wincey Spider

Aims of the rhyme or song

This is a traditional action rhyme which is useful for revising prepositions, animal names and weather.

Lexis: *up, down, rain, sunshine.*

Extension lexis: *What's the weather like today? raining, cloudy, windy, foggy, snowing, sunny, hot, cold.*

The rhyme

'Incey 'Wincey 'Spider 'climbed 'up the 'spout,
'Down 'came the 'rain,
And 'washed poor 'Incey 'out.
'Out 'came the 'sun
And 'dried up 'all the 'rain
So 'Incey 'Wincey 'Spider
'Climbed 'up the 'spout a'gain.
Note: This rhyme can be adapted to use the present tense if you wish.

Presentation

1 Basic procedure: using your coursebook

- Use a page from your coursebook to talk about the weather. Ask the children to point to a picture of a sunny day. Tell the children to look at the weather outside the classroom. Point to the sky and ask them *What's the weather like today?* Ask them *Is it hot today or is it cold today?* Mime *hot* (by pretending to wipe sweat from your forehead) and *cold* (by shivering and chattering your teeth). Now answer the question yourself *It's sunny/cloudy*, etc. Repeat the question and let the children answer in English, e.g. *It's raining today.*

- Point to other pictures in the coursebook where the weather is different, e.g. cold, snowing, foggy, raining. Put the children into pairs and ask them to point to different pictures and ask and answer the question.

  A: *What's the weather like today?*
  B: *It's cold and raining./It's hot and sunny.*

  Reverse the roles so that both children ask the question and reply.

2 Class activity: the Incey Wincey Spider game

Materials needed: black card, scissors and string, copies of PHOTOCOPIABLE PAGE 3.

- Ask the children to stick the photocopiable page to the black card. They cut the spider out and attach the string to the top of the spider.

- Find a large area in the gym or the playground. Divide the class into two teams in two lines. Give one team the name *Incey* and the other team the name *Wincey*. Each group has their spiders on the end of a piece of string and faces the other team.

- Pretend that the space in-between is a river. The Wincey team ask the Incey team *Please Mr Incey, can we cross the river?* The first person in the Incey team has to reply *Only if your name has the letter A in it.* Explain to the children that they may go over to the other team if this is correct.

- Reverse the question so that the Incey team asks *Please Mr Wincey, can we cross the river?* The first person in the Wincey team replies *Only if your name has the letter B/C, etc. in it.* They must choose a letter and if this applies to anyone in the other team they may cross the river with their spiders.

- Continue until all the children have crossed the river at least once.

Practice

1 Saying the rhyme

- Say the whole rhyme to the children, miming the actions with your hands. For the spider going up, demonstrate how to put the right hand thumb on the left hand little finger and rotate the hands so that the right hand little finger is placed on the left hand thumb. Continue this up into the air. Use your fingers to mime the rain falling. Put both hands out and up in the air and wave to mime the sun. Then repeat the actions for the first line as the spider climbs up again.

● Say each line with actions again, asking the children to repeat each line after you while doing the actions. Repeat the whole rhyme again until they can say it confidently, with the actions.

2 Exploiting the rhyme

Divide the class into two groups. One group mimes the actions and the other group says the words to the rhyme. Change over roles and repeat.

7 Chant: Nobody loves me, everybody hates me

Aims of the chant

This is a traditional chant which is useful for revising feelings, animal foods and opposite adjectives. It is useful to extend the lexis for these areas. It is possible to add actions to the words.

Lexis: *love, hate; big, little; fat, thin; long, short.*

Extension lexis: *sad, happy; angry, scared; a bird/cat/dog/cow eats …; What does a … eat?*

The chant

'Nobody 'loves 'me,
'Everybody 'hates 'me,
I 'think I'll 'go and 'eat 'worms.

'Big fat 'squishy 'ones,
'Little thin 'skinny 'ones,
'See how they 'wriggle and 'squirm.

'Bite their 'heads off,
'Schlurp! They're 'lovely,
'Throw their 'tails a'way.

'Nobody 'knows,
How 'big I 'grow,
On 'worms 'three 'times a 'day.

Preparation

1 Basic procedure: using your coursebook

● Find a page in your coursebook which shows a picture of birds and animals. Point to one of the animals or birds and ask the children *What does a … eat?* The children reply e.g. *A bird eats worms./A cat eats fish or meat./A dog eats meat./A cow eats grass.*

● In pairs, Child A asks the question and Child B replies. Then change roles.

Adapting for higher levels

Higher-level pupils can extend the animals and the types of food which they eat.

2 Opposites: *fat, thin; long, short*

● Draw a fat worm and a thin worm on the board. Point to the fat worm. Ask the children *What kind of worm is this?* Tell them *It's a fat worm.* Point to the thin worm. Ask the children *What kind of worm is this?* Tell them *It's a thin worm.* Point to the worms again in turn. The children repeat *It's a fat worm, It's a thin worm.*

● Draw a long and a short worm and repeat the exercise.

3 Class activity: expressions and feelings

● Mime. Ask the children *How do I look when I am sad?* and mime a sad face. Tell the children to pull a sad face and say *I'm sad.* Then do the same with other adjectives: *happy, angry* and *scared.*

● Write the four words for these feelings on the board and draw faces with the relevant expression (SEE PAGE 60). Ask the children to draw semi-circles and to add wings and beaks. Tell the children to fill in the expressions on the birds' faces, as left.

Presentation and practice

1 Saying the chant

● Read the chant to the class, miming the actions and feelings. Explain that this is a story of a bird who is not happy so he eats a very big worm. Ask the children what they do when they are not happy (but explain that they must never try and eat worms!). Repeat each line so that the children say the words and pretend to eat worms.

● Divide the class into four groups; each group says one verse. Change the groups and repeat the rhyme so that they say another verse. Continue until each group has said all four verses. Repeat the rhyme until all the class knows the words.

2 Extending the chant for higher level students: adjectives

● Ask the children to make up another verse about a long worm and a short worm – like the second verse. Ask the class to illustrate the rhyme in the shapes of worms using the descriptions in the rhyme.

● Ask them to draw other worms using the opposites *long* and *short* which they talked about in Preparation activity 2. Ask them to draw worms with expressions sad, happy, angry, scared.

3 Exploiting the chant: memory game

● For this activity you'll need two small squares of paper per child. Divide the class into four groups. Ask each group to draw either a worm or a bird to illustrate each of the following words: *long, short, fat, thin* (for worms); *big, little, happy, sad, angry, scared* (for birds).

● Ask the children to put all the pictures on the table or floor face down. Mix them up.

● In turn, each child turns two pieces of paper over and tries to find two pictures illustrating the same word. If they don't find a pair, they must turn the papers back over and let the next child have a go. When all the pictures are gone, the group with the most pairs wins the game.

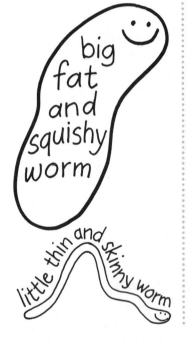

T A S K

1 Look at the activities contained in this chapter. Identify how you could use these with the content of your coursebook.
2 Look through the action chants and their possible extensions/exploitation and select one which supplements your current lessons. Did the activities work as you expected? If not, why? Did something go wrong? How can you improve the activity for your class?

CHAPTER 4

Things to make and use throughout the school year

"What are the practical benefits of these resources?"

In this chapter you will find ideas for teaching resources that you can prepare inexpensively and easily, for later use with your classes. You will also find ideas for things that the children themselves can make as projects that are ongoing throughout the year. The criteria for these resources are as follows.

- They are cheap and do not require expensive materials.
- They have linguistic relevance.
- They reflect the needs of the class.
- They reflect the content of your coursebook.
- They have an on-going relevance.
- They help provide variety, broadening both the focus and the linguistic content of class activity.

"What are the pedagogical aims behind making these resources?"

The pedagogical aims behind making and using these resources are as follows.

- They reflect and develop useful educational skills, both in terms of linguistic and cognitive development.
- They help to develop a sense of child autonomy and identity.
- They give the children a sense of progress and achievement.
- They are achievable by all the children in the class.
- They help to establish links between English and the children's own experience, lifting English out of the realms of academic activity.
- They are a genuine opportunity for personalisation. They allow the children to use English to express their own opinions.
- They provide older children with the opportunity for contextualised writing activities.
- They set up a valuable source of information for you to consult when you want to evaluate an individual child's progress.
- They provide an excellent opportunity for the children to learn by doing something that is enjoyable in itself.
- They can be used to celebrate achievement and to help build positive attitudes within the class.
- They have an aim and purpose. They provide a meaningful context for activity.

Look back at the ideas contained in this introduction. Do they form part of the pedagogical requirements for primary teaching in your country? Which ones are most appropriate for your situation?

1 Making flashcards

There are many sets of FLASHCARDS available commercially. The ideas in this section are not intended to replace these. They are designed to help you supplement existing sets of FLASHCARDS or to bring old sets up to date with your coursebook materials. For suggestions on how to use FLASHCARDS effectively in the classroom see *An Introduction to Teaching English to Children*, in the same series.

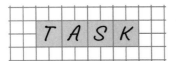

Write down four reasons why you think FLASHCARDS are a useful classroom resource and then compare your answers with the ideas below.

"Why are flashcards a useful classroom resource?"

FLASHCARDS, whether home-made or bought, are a useful resource for every teacher. They allow the children to associate pictures with FOCUS LEXIS in isolation. Making your own FLASHCARDS has the following benefits.

- They are a cheap resource for the teacher to use.
- They can be used in games to reinforce and consolidate FOCUS LEXIS.
- They are a resource that can be made to reflect the needs of the class, as the school year progresses.
- They are a resource that can be built upon over several years and a way to supplement existing FLASHCARDS.
- They are a resource that can be shared by other teachers.

When to make your flashcards

Decide in advance when you are going to make your FLASHCARDS. The easiest way to make them is before you start a new topic with your class. This means that you only have to make a limited number at any one time. You might like to make the FLASHCARDS in co-operation with other English teachers. This would mean that you had a shared set. It would also make the process of formulating the set of FLASHCARDS quicker. Make sure that you have all the materials to hand and that you have the time necessary to make them properly.

How to store your flashcards

It is a good idea to keep them all in one place and to store them in a systematic and ordered way. If your coursebook covers ten topics in a year, you might like to have ten large envelopes, each labelled with the title of the topics covered in the coursebook. These sets could then be stored in a box or file in the staff room, or at home.

How to decide which flashcards to make

You can use the wordlists or language boxes found in your teacher's book or in the pupil's materials to identify which FLASHCARDS to make.

How to make your flashcards

1 Basic principles and procedures

You don't have to be an artist to produce effective FLASHCARDS. Before you start, make a list of the FLASHCARDS you want to include then follow these basic steps.

- Use good quality card, and make all the FLASHCARDS the same size.
- Make sure that they are big enough to be seen by children sitting at the back of the classroom.

- Make sure the pictures on each card are big and bold. Detailed pictures will be less clear to see.
- Write the name of each FOCUS WORD on the back of the FLASHCARDS so that you know what is on the card without turning it round; and make sure that the words are big enough to be seen from the back of the class.
- At this stage you could cover the cards with clear laminate paper (sticky-back plastic), but this is not essential and it can be time consuming and can add to the cost.

As an alternative, you could ask your class to make the FLASHCARDS for particular word groups. Prepare the pieces of card beforehand and make sure each child knows exactly what he/she has to do.

2 Easy to draw: numbers, colours and alphabet

Even for the worst artist in the world numbers, colours and letters of the alphabet are all easy FLASHCARDS to make.

- For numbers draw the number on the front of the card and write the number words on the back.
- For colours draw a shape and colour it in. Write the colour words on the back.
- For letters of the alphabet write the letters in capitals and small letters on the front. On the back of each card write a FOCUS WORD that the children will be able to find in their coursebook. For example, for the letter A, find a word that appears in the coursebook, e.g. *apple*, *acrobat*, etc.

3 Other sources: magazines, brochures and catalogues

Instead of drawing your own pictures, look through and find pictures in magazines which reflect the words you want to cover. You might like to find several examples, so that you have a selection of pictures to choose from. Then follow these steps.

- Pull out the pages with the pictures on and put to one side.
- Choose which picture you are going to use from each selection of pictures. Remember that big pictures are best.
- Cut out the pictures you have chosen. Try not to include any background detail, so that the image is as clear as possible.
- Stick the pictures on to the prepared cards.

Adapting for older children

Older children could help you to find the pictures to use for the FLASHCARDS. Let the children work in groups. Give each group a selection of magazines, brochures and old catalogues, then tell the children which pictures to look for.

4 Supplementing existing sets of flashcards

You might already have a set of FLASHCARDS, but find that it does not cover all the lexis you need to reflect your coursebook. You can always make up cards to supplement this set. Just make sure that you make the new cards the same size as the existing ones. Use any of the ideas outlined in sections 1 to 3 above.

5 Recycling old sets of flashcards

You might already have a set of FLASHCARDS, but feel that they are now rather old and used. In this case you can cut up the old pictures and remount them on new card, supplementing missing words with ideas outlined in sections 1 to 3 above.

2 Making personal dictionaries

Many coursebooks include a picture dictionary. However, the type of dictionary activities described here offer a more extensive opportunity for the children to personalise their own lexical development.

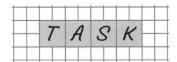

Think of three reasons why personal dictionaries are a useful classroom resource. Then compare your ideas with the following features.

"Why are personal dictionaries a useful classroom resource?"

Being able to use a dictionary is a useful educational skill to develop. It helps to develop a sense of child autonomy and self help in the classroom. Creating their own personal dictionaries gives the children a sense of progress and helps them to identify their growing vocabulary bank. Dictionaries help to reinforce the lexis presented and practised in the coursebook. They are a resource that can be made throughout the school year, as an ongoing project. They can even be used and built upon over several years.

When to make a personal dictionary

When to start making personal dictionaries depends on the age and cognitive development of the children in your class. It is not necessary for the children to be able to write, but they do need to be able to recognise the relevance of categorising information. It is probably best to establish a regular pattern of dictionary-making with your class, using some of the following.

- You might like to do this as a word-collection exercise at the end of each coursebook topic or unit.
- You could dedicate five minutes of each lesson to dictionary work.
- You could have a dictionary-making slot once a week or once every two weeks.
- You might like to use dictionary-making activities to quieten the children down, e.g. after games or more physical activities.

Whichever option you choose, make sure that the children have the necessary materials and time to concentrate on the activity. Always ensure that the children know how to record the words. ◆ SEE SECTION 5 ON PAGE 42

How to organise the dictionaries

It is a good idea to choose how you want to organise the dictionary before you start. Do you want it to be categorised in lexical sets according to topic (animals, family, food, colours, etc.) or do you want to organise it alphabetically (A, B, C, etc.)?

Look at how your coursebook is organised. If it is organised into units with a strong topic focus, it would be a good idea to make lexically organised dictionaries. If it does not have strong topic focus, it is probably a better idea to organise it alphabetically.

Before you start a dictionary session with your class, make sure that you are aware of the words you think the children should include. You can check the language by looking in the unit wordlists or language boxes in your teacher's book, or by going through the pages of the coursebook.

Note: You might like to use a lexically organised dictionary for the first two years of English and then change to an alphabetically organised dictionary.

How to make personal dictionaries

1 Basic procedures

The first thing you need to decide is how you want the children to organise their dictionary and what they're going to use as a dictionary.

- You can ask the children to use an exercise book dedicated to dictionary work.
- Alternatively, you could ask the children to use an A4 file, or to make a simple book made up of pages fastened with staples or by punching holes in the edge of the pages and attaching with string.

2 Lexical dictionaries

For lexical set dictionaries, we suggest that you ask the children to use four pages per set. You will not need to tell them the individual sets until they cover them in their coursebook work.

3 Alphabetical dictionaries

For alphabetically organised dictionaries you could tell the children to give two pages to each letter, with only one page for Q, and one page for X, Y, Z. They'll therefore need a total of 46 pages. The first page dedicated to each letter could have a border made up of the focus letter. Give each child a copy of PHOTOCOPIABLE PAGE 4, containing the letters of the alphabet, and ask them to colour the letters and stick them in their dictionary book.

4 Layout and presentation

Whether you decide to make a lexically organised or an alphabetically organised dictionary with the children, it is important to remember that dictionaries for young children should never just be lists of words. There are lots of ways to make the individual pages attractive to look at. The most important consideration is space: the more cramped the words are the less appealing the dictionary will look.

Another important consideration is the use of colour. Children are attracted to and like to use colour. So let them decorate the pages of their dictionaries, in order to make them as attractive and as personal as possible.

Try to instil a sense of pride and care in what the children do by making sure that you look at what they have done and give lots of praise.

5 Different ways to record words

Some children, but not all, like to draw. To ensure that all children are catered for it is probably a good idea to give a variety of ways in which to record the words in the dictionary activities. Let the children draw things that are quick and easy to record. If class time is limited you can also encourage the children to draw their items in pencil and to colour them in at home.

Another way to record dictionary words is to give the children old magazines, brochures and catalogues. The children can find pictures to represent the FOCUS WORDS, cut them out and stick them in their dictionaries.

6 Writing dictionary words

In many cases children learning English are not encouraged to write much before the age of about nine. However, as long as the children can identify pictures and write the names of individual words, they can begin to make a picture dictionary of their own. You can write the words on the board, for the children to copy under the corresponding picture. Alternatively you can ask the children to copy the words from their coursebook.

Adapting for higher levels

With higher levels you might like them to write short phrases under the pictures in their dictionary, e.g. *This is a plane*. Or they could record personal information, e.g. *I've got a skateboard*.

7 How to store the personal dictionaries

You might like the children to keep their dictionaries at home. However, you could have a shelf where you keep all the dictionaries. Make a sign saying *Our dictionaries* and encourage the children to use them for reference during class activities. Keeping them at school will also avoid the problem of the children leaving them at home.

8 Homework option

You could ask the children to complete their dictionary-making activities for homework. This would allow the children to take more time and care in their development.

3 Making personal scrapbooks

Personal scrapbooks are an enjoyable and worthwhile activity to carry out with the children. They are a flexible resource that can be tailored to fit the interests and development of the children in your class.

Cover the list below. Think of four reasons why personal scrapbooks are a useful classroom resource to develop. Then compare your ideas with those below.

"Why are personal scrapbooks a useful class resource?"

- They help to establish links between English and the children's own experience, lifting English out of the realms of academic activity.
- They are a genuine opportunity for personalisation. They allow the children to use English to express their own opinions.
- They allow the children to record information about themselves in parallel with the topics covered throughout the school year.
- They provide older children or pupils at a higher level with the opportunity for contextualised writing activities.
- They provide a task that can be used and built upon over several years.
- They are a valuable source of information for you to consult when you want to evaluate an individual child's progress.
- They are something that the children can take home and show their parents.
- They provide an excellent opportunity for the children to learn by doing something that is enjoyable in itself.

Using personal scrapbooks for evaluation

Scrapbooks provide you with an excellent opportunity to see how the child has developed and approached the different activities you have given them throughout the school year. Each child's personal scrapbook will reflect the child's own ability and progress. Set aside a regular time to look at the scrapbook activities and use work from the scrapbooks to celebrate achievement. Put individual children's work on the class noticeboard (SEE PAGE 46). But remember to praise effort and presentation as well as linguistic competence. Look at the scrapbooks after each activity. Make a note of the areas the children have most difficulty with and then repeat the coursebook exercises that focus on the language points which they find most difficult.

When to make personal scrapbooks

Follow the procedures outlined in *When to make a personal dictionary*, PAGE 40.

How to organise the content of a personal scrapbook

Look at how the coursebook you are using is organised. If it is topic-led try to think of ways of personalising the content. The chart on PAGE 44 contains some basic ideas you might like to explore.

Finding the right content

Think about whether you want the children to write anything. It is important that any written context should match the content of the activity. We record information in a wide variety of forms, e.g. titles, slogans, messages, letters, recipes, menus, stories, cartoons, speech bubbles, newspapers, adverts, road signs, shop signs, words on clothing, labels, lists, diaries, computers, maps, greeting cards, on transport, etc.

Topic	Language ideas	Content ideas
My school	*This is my …* *There's a …* *His/Her name's …* *Who do you sit next to?* *Who's your best friend?*	Make a plan of the classroom
School subjects and days of the week	*When have we got …?*	Make your school timetable
My family	*This is my …* *He/She has got …* Colours Numbers Family lexis	Who are the people in your family? Make a monster or an animal family
My home	*My house has got …* *I live in … Street.* Prepositions of place: *in on under next to behind between* *In my street there's a …* (shops lexis) *In my bedroom there's a …* (furniture and toy lexis)	What's your house like? Make a plan of your bedroom or house Make a plan of your street
Animals	*I love …* *My favourite animals are …* Colours Descriptive lexis such as *feathers, fur, scales*	What's your favourite animal? Think about animals that: live on the land/in the sea, etc. can fly/swim/run, etc. eat grass/meat, etc. live in the sea/trees, etc.
My hobbies	*I love …ing.* *My favourite sport/hobby is …* *After school I like …*	What's your favourite sport/hobby? What do you like doing after after school?
My life	Days of the week Present simple Past simple Adverbs of frequency: *I usually/ sometimes/often/never,* etc.	Write or draw a diary for one week Think about what you do at the weekend/on schooldays
My clothes	Clothes lexis Seasons Carnival, Christmas Clothes for a day out in the mountains/on the beach, etc.	Categorise clothes for different seasons Think about clothes for different occasions and pastimes
Weather	Seasons Days of the week Months of the year *When it's … I like …ing.*	Make a diary of the weather

Adapting for older children or higher levels

Older children or higher-level pupils might like to write more extensively about the things they have drawn in their scrapbooks. In this case make sure that you provide the children with a clear writing model to follow. You can do this in different ways.

- Write a gap-fill description on the board, e.g. *When it's sunny I like …*
- Write a gap-fill description on a piece of paper that can then be photocopied and given to the children to complete. The children can then cut this out and stick it in their scrapbooks, e.g. *This is my family. I've got … brothers and … sisters. My mum's name is … and my dad's name is …*
- Write word trees on the board for the children to use, e.g.

This is my	brother. sister. mum. etc.

He's She's	got	brown blonde black	hair.

Ideas for different activities to include in making a personal scrapbook

It is a good idea to give the children a variety of ways of recording their information in their scrapbooks. This will help the children to identify different ways and contexts for using text.

- Writing the date: put the date on the board each time the children use their scrapbooks; this will help to make it into a kind of diary.
- Picture poems: encourage the children to write simple poems to reflect the content of the activity.

- Letters and postcards: the children write to a friend or one of the characters from the coursebook.
- Invitations: the children make an invitation to invite a classmate, character from the coursebook, or a favourite cartoon character to a special occasion.
- Recipes: the children make up recipes for special occasions.
- Word pictures: the children make word pictures, e.g.

- The children design a poster.
- The children make a comic strip. They can draw and fill in fill in speech bubbles.
- The children make 'behind the door' or 'pocket' activities.

Homework option

Any of the ideas contained in this section can be set for homework.

4 Making a class noticeboard

Think of four reasons why a class noticeboard could be a useful classroom resource to develop. Compare your answers with the ideas outlined below.

"Why is it useful to have a class noticeboard in the classroom?"

- A noticeboard is something from other areas of children's school life.
- It is a way of bringing English into the sphere of the children's own lives and experience.
- It is a resource that can be made to reflect the interests of the class, as the school year progresses.
- It can be used to celebrate achievement and to help build positive attitudes within the class.
- It is a resource that can be used and built upon over several years.
- It provides a visually stimulating focus point in the classroom that will remind the children of English at other times.
- The noticeboard can reflect and develop the following educational values: co-operation, finding out and recording information, learner autonomy and classroom organisation, group identity.

When to make your class noticeboard

This is an activity that you can start at the beginning of the school year, at the beginning of a new term, or at any point in the year.

Where to have your class noticeboard

Ideally you would have a class noticeboard in the children's own classroom or the room the children use the most. If, however, the children move from class to class you could organise a noticeboard in public areas of the school, in the corridors, the canteen, the hall, etc.

How to organise your class noticeboard

It is a good idea to have an area of the classroom that can be dedicated to the noticeboard. In this way the children will become accustomed to its role and existence. It is important to remember that a noticeboard is not merely a display, but that it has the function of being a source for a range of information.

- If you don't already have a suitable board in the classroom, here are two very simple ways of creating a noticeboard.
  1 Stick up strips of coloured paper or card to form a noticeboard area.
  2 Stick up four large sheets of coloured paper to form a noticeboard area.

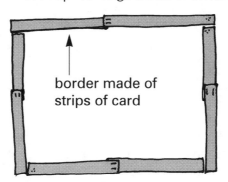

border made of strips of card

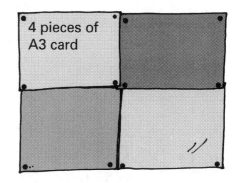

4 pieces of A3 card

The golden rules

There are four golden rules to follow when developing a class noticeboard.

1 Put the noticeboard at the eye level of the children in the class.
2 Include a variety of things that have visual appeal.
3 Change some part of the board at regular intervals.
4 Use it!

What to include on your class noticeboard

There are many things that you might like to include on an English noticeboard. Here are just a few ideas, but feel free to include any others you think of – just make sure that you can think of a way of making them relevant to English studies.

1 Birthday chart

Ask all the children to bring in a photograph of themselves. Make a chart of when the children's birthdays are. Put the chart on the noticeboard. Whenever it is the week of somebody's birthday, put their photo up on the noticeboard. Sing 'Happy Birthday' to the children.

2 Monitors' chart

If you assign different children to be responsible for carrying out certain tasks in the classroom, you might like to make a chart for the class noticeboard. The types of monitor activity might be:

… handing out or collecting up books and other resources
… making sure the class is clean and tidy at the end of lessons
… making sure that all chairs are put under the desks
… cleaning the board
… writing the date on the board
… helping disabled children to leave the class and carry out class activities.

You can organise a monitors' chart at the beginning of each new term. Look at the register for the class and allocate a task to two or three children at a time. Divide the length of time the children are responsible for a given task by the number of months or weeks in the school year.

3 Show case

Use the noticeboard to display pieces of work done by individual children. This is a good opportunity to celebrate achievement. Remember, though, not always to display the same child's work. Make sure that everybody is included at some point in the school year. It might not always be linguistic or academic excellence that you want to praise, sometimes it might be effort or good illustration.

4 Special days and festivals

You can also use the noticeboard to put up information relating to forthcoming festivals, special days and events. If you do this, make sure that you include some element relevant to the English classroom. The simplest way to do this is to write labels in English. If you have access to the materials you could also put up pictures of corresponding festivals and events in English-speaking countries.

5 English around us

The children might be aware of English words that are used in their own language. You could encourage the children to bring in English words that they have found on food wrappers, games, adverts, signs and notices, clothes, etc. If you cannot use the original source for these words, get the children to draw pictures of them. Put them on the noticeboard in a category of their own.

6 Weather chart

◆ SEE *MAKING A WEATHER CHART* PAGE 54

7 Newsflash

You could include a section on the noticeboard where you can record information of personal relevance to individual children. For example, if a child has a new baby brother or sister, they might like this news to be acknowledged in class. Other things might be new pets, achievement in other areas of school life, sporting achievement, moving house, weddings, etc.

8 Unit marker

You can encourage a sense of child autonomy and learner training by including a simple unit marker. This can be done by having a permanent note on the board: *We're doing Unit …*, and writing/sticking the unit numbers from the coursebook on the board as appropriate.

> **T A S K** Look at the ideas contained in this chapter so far and consider which would hold the biggest appeal for the children in your class. Choose two ideas as a starting point. Then choose one more that can be introduced at a later date.

5 Making instant puppets

"Why are puppets useful in the primary EFL classroom?"

Puppets can be used in stories, songs, chants, ROLEPLAY and pairwork. There are several pedagogical and linguistic aims behind using puppets.

- For motivation. It is fun so the children will try to speak or listen without inhibition.
- For meaning. The children will try to understand what is happening so they listen with a purpose.
- For fluency. In the desire to communicate with the puppets, the children will build up a flow of language and learn new words.
- For communication. Puppets make even the shyest child become involved, as the child is participating 'out of character', i.e. using a different character from their own, or communicating with 'someone' outside the normal class environment.
- For cross-curricular activities. Puppets can be used in most topic areas of the curriculum.
- To teach vocabulary used in a story or ROLEPLAY; parts of the face: *eyes, nose, mouth, ears, hair, whiskers*, etc.
- To teach language for making puppets, e.g. verbs: *to colour, to draw*, etc.

How to make instant puppets

Materials needed: card; scissors; coloured felt-tip pens; glue; scraps of fabric, ribbon and wool.

Time needed: 15–20 minutes per puppet.

The most important thing to remember when making a puppet for language teaching is the fact that the features of the character play an important part in bringing out the person behind the puppet. You might consider copying (and enlarging) the illustrations on the next page to show students what sort of puppets they can make.

1 Hand puppets

- Draw a face on your clenched fist. By moving the thumb up and down you have a mouth to speak.

3 Paper bag puppets

- Draw a face to show an expression on a paper bag and tie it around the wrist with help.

5 Toilet roll puppets

- Attach a ruler or a stick to the inside of a toilet roll.
- Draw the eyes, nose and mouth with coloured felt tip pens and add hair if necessary.

7 Yoghurt pot or plastic cup puppets

- Use a clean empty yoghurt pot or plastic cup. Turn it upside down and draw the face on the pot.
- Attach it to a ruler or a stick and add hair if necessary.

2 Wooden spoon puppets

- Use a wooden spoon and draw a face on the back with coloured felt tip pens.
- Decorate the head of the puppet with strips of wool for hair. Use scraps of material to wrap around the handle for a cloak, etc.

4 Sock puppets

- Put a sock on your left hand so that the fingers are in the toe area and the thumb is in the heel of the sock. This forms the mouth of the puppet.
- Draw eyes and a nose with felt tip pen or glue buttons on for eyes. Stick cardboard ears to the back of the sock. They can be in the form of dog with long ears or a cat with small pointed ears and whiskers. A green sock can be used to make a crocodile.

6 Worm or caterpillar puppets

- A strip of stiff paper or card can be made into a concertina by folding it backwards and forwards at 5cm intervals and adding two thin strips of card and a face at one end.

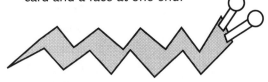

8 Finger puppets

- Draw a face on a piece of card and stick it on your finger or draw around a shape and add pieces of material, etc. to make features.

How to use your instant puppets

1 Introduce the idea

Make an example before the lesson. Take the puppet character into the classroom, introduce the children to it, then encourage them to talk directly to the puppet. Elicit language by asking questions, e.g. Say *Hello, what's my name?*

2 Adaptation for a story called 'Witchy and Itchy'

This and point 3 below are both specific uses of puppets.

- Make a forgetful witch with a yoghurt pot, black card and material.
- Make up a story first, e.g. about what Witchy puts in her magic pot to make a new spell. The children should remember what she puts in her magic pot.
- Tell the children *Witchy needs help in collecting special ingredients for her magic spell, which she has forgotten how to make.*
- Using the puppet, ask the children *What must she put in the magic pot?* They will ask her questions or disagree with her.
- Demonstrate how to make the puppets for Witchy and for Itchy, the cat.
- The children can make their own witches or cats.
- In pairs they can act out what Witchy is going to put in her spell and what Itchy replies.

3 For practice using *Wh*- questions or *yes/no* questions

- Present an exchange at the beginning of the lesson using two finger puppets.

  Puppet A: *Why are you writing?*
  Puppet B: *I'm writing to my friend.*
  Puppet A: *What are you writing?*
  Puppet B: *I'm writing a letter.*

- Negatives can be made in the exchange as one puppet contradicts another.

  Puppet A: *You're writing.*
  Puppet B: *No, I'm not writing, I'm reading.*

- Children can draw a face on the first finger of their left hand.
- Divide the class into pairs. They can repeat this exercise and the dialogue can be extended if necessary.

6 Making simple masks

"Why use masks in the primary EFL classroom?"

Play-acting behind a mask helps the children to become aware of the sound of the foreign language, practising new vocabulary, etc. There are several pedagogical aims behind using masks.

- For motivation: They are fun, so the children will try to speak or listen without inhibition.
- For communication. Listening and responding to other children wearing a mask helps to involve even shy children.
- For use in stories, songs, chants, ROLEPLAY and drama. Masks can be used to dramatise even the most simple situations.
- For language familiarisation.

The linguistic aims are to teach names of farm and circus animals: *pig, lion, elephant, rabbit, crocodile, cat, frog,* etc. and verbs: *to cut, to fold, to glue, to stick, to colour.*

How to make simple masks

Materials needed: white or coloured paper plates; felt tip pens; SELLOTAPE; glue; scissors; small yoghurt cartons; strips of coloured paper; 2 pieces of string, 20 cm long; stapler (if possible).

Time needed: 15 minutes for each mask.

Simple masks can also be made from cardboard or paper bags. They can be on sticks and just cover the eyes. They can be decorated with coloured materials and they can be beautiful, funny, frightening or mysterious.

Basic paper plate mask

- Hold the paper plate up to the face and mark where the eyes, nose and mouth are with a pen. It is best for the teacher to cut the holes for the children.

- Attach a piece of string to both sides of the mask with SELLOTAPE or through a small hole and tie a knot. Use the string to tie the mask round the child's head.

1 To make a Pig mask →

- Glue a small yoghurt pot to the centre of the plate and draw two dots in the middle of the base.

- Cut two ears from the card and glue them to the top of the plate.

- Ask the children what noise a pig makes: say *Oink, oink.*

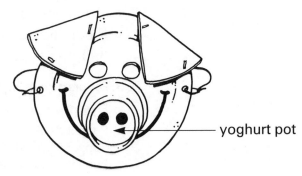

—————— yoghurt pot

← 2 To make a Lion mask

- Colour or paint the paper plate yellow.

- To make a mane, cut a strip of yellow paper 5cm wide and measure the circumference of the plate. Cut slits along the side of the paper and glue the paper all around the edge of the mask.

- Draw and colour the lion's eyes, nose, mouth, and whiskers.

- Ask the children what noise a lion makes: say *Roar.*

3 To make an Elephant mask →

- Colour or paint the plate grey. Cut out a trunk, large elephant ears and tusks from card. Stick these onto the paper plate and decorate.

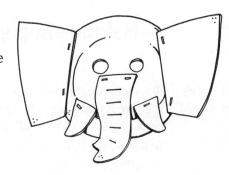

← 4 To make a Rabbit mask

- Colour or paint the plate grey or brown. Cut out long rabbit ears and paint whiskers on the plate. Colour the eyes and nose.

← 5 To make a Cat mask

- Colour or paint the paper plate light brown.
- Cut out two cat's ears and attach to the plate. Cut out a red tongue and stick it inside the mouth.
- Draw cat's eyes and a nose on the plate, and glue long whiskers to it.
- Ask the children what noise a cat makes: say *Miaow*.

6 To make a Clown mask →

- Draw and cut out a large hat for the clown.
- Cut yellow or orange paper in long strips for hair and glue this to the sides of the plate. Glue the hat on above the hair.
- Draw the clown's eyes, nose and large red mouth.

← 7 To make a Frog mask/puppet

- Colour two paper plates green.
- Cut out two large eyes and stick them to the first plate. Fold the second plate in half.
- Stick the folded plate below the eyes on the first plate.
- Show the children how to hold the plate up in front of their mouths and open and close it as they speak.
- For a puppet attach the eyes to the folded plate only.

How to use your simple masks

Adaptation for *The farmer's in his den* ◆ SEE PAGE 23

- Make a mask of a farmer using a paper plate, and then do the following: cut white paper into long strips to make whiskers and stick them below his nose for a moustache and a beard. Draw and cut a hat out of brown card. Draw and cut out a fork, and stick the fork handle behind the plate.
- Divide the class into four or six groups.
- Each group makes a mask to represent the animals from the song *The farmer's in his den*, i.e. cows, cats, horses, dogs, hens, pigs.
- Sing the song together.
- Ask each group to sing the verse about their animal.
- All the class sings the chorus between each verse and changes the name of the animals.
- You can stop before each verse and point to the next group of animals and say *Let's have the sheep next. What sound does a sheep make?* Repeat using each group of animals.

Adaptation for a Frog mask

Lexis: *up/down*, *high/low*, numbers 1–5.

- Show the class how to make a frog mask and ask five children to come to the front of the class and mime the actions.

- All the class says the following traditional rhyme.

  Five little frogs sitting on a well
  One looked up and down he fell!
  Frogs jumped high, frogs jumped low;
  And four little frogs searched high and low …
  … But they couldn't find him!
  Four little frogs, etc.
  (Repeat for three, two, and one)
  No little frogs sitting on the well,
  Because they all looked up and down they fell!
  Their mother jumped high, their mother jumped low;
  The mother frog searched high and low …
  … And she found all of them!

- Change the group at the front of the class and say the rhyme again.

- Divide the class into five groups. Each group can say a verse and everyone says the last verse.

7 Making a weather chart

"Why is a weather chart useful in the primary EFL classroom?"

A weather chart is useful in the following ways.

- It can be used to teach language and vocabulary involving the weather.
- It can be used for a weather topic.
- It can be used to extend stories and poems about the weather.
- It is a resource that can be used daily.
- It can be re-used if separate cards are made.
- It is a cheap resource for the teacher to use.
- It can be used when teaching other language areas, e.g. days of the week, months of the year and seasons.

When to use a weather chart

- The topic of weather is often part of the primary curriculum and can be studied on a daily basis.
- A simple weather chart can be completed by individual children, by groups, or by the whole class.
- It can be drawn by the teacher on a large sheet of paper and attached to the wall and filled in daily. Or it can be copied by the children and filled in daily.

How to make a weather chart

1 For a classroom wall chart

Materials needed: a large sheet of card or paper, coloured felt tip pens, strips of stiff card, BLU-TACK or SELLOTAPE.

- Look at the chart on PHOTOCOPIABLE PAGE 5. Copy the chart and stick it onto a large sheet of stiff card, and draw/stick the symbols at the side of the chart. Then ask the children to fill it in by copying the symbols.
- To re-use the chart make separate cards of the symbols for the children to stick on each day rather than drawing on the chart.

2 For individual charts

Materials needed: a sheet of A4 paper or a page in an exercise book, coloured pens or pencils.

- Copy the chart onto the board or photocopy a sheet for each child. If they are drawing it themselves, ask the children to copy the chart from the board.

Activities using the weather chart

1 The days of the week

Linguistic aims: to teach the lexis for the days of the week and questions *What …? When …?*

- Ask the children *What day is it today?* Accept the right day in L1 and tell the children the correct day in English.
- Read the names of the days of the week to the class. Then ask the children to say them with you.
- Divide the class into two groups. One group says the days *Monday, Wednesday, Friday, Sunday*. The other group says the days *Tuesday, Thursday, Saturday*.
- Point to each group alternately and say the days in the correct order.

2 What is the weather like today?

Linguistic aims: to teach the lexis *It's* + adjectives (*snowy/cold, rainy/wet, sunny/hot, cloudy/cool, cloudy/warm, stormy, windy, foggy, misty*).

- Ask the children *What's the weather like today?* Look out of the window.
- Repeat the question.
- Tell the children to point to the symbol on the chart.
- Accept the correct adjective in L1 and reply, e.g. *Yes, it's sunny*.
- Tell the children to draw the correct symbol on their own chart or ask one child to come out to the classroom chart and fill in the correct symbol under the right day.
- Ask the class *What's the weather like today?*
- Point to the chart and if it is raining, say *It's wet*; if it is sunny, say *It's hot*.

3 The months of the year

Linguistic aims: to teach the months of the year and questions: *Which …? When …?*

- Write the names of the months on the board and ask the class *Which month is it?*
- Point to the correct month and say, e.g. *It's January*.

- Tell the class to repeat after you *It's January* and say the whole list together with the class.
- Divide the class into two groups and chant the months.

4 Extension activities using your weather chart

Linguistic aims: to teach the dates of the month, *What is the date today?* and the ordinal numbers to 31st.

- Write the numbers on the board.
- Ask the class *What is the date today?* and point to the correct date.
- Ask the children to say the numbers with you.
- Divide the class into two groups. Group A says the odd numbers. Group B says the even numbers.
- Change roles and repeat.
- Ask the class *When is your birthday?*
- In pairs they can repeat the question and reply *My birthday is on the …* (12th June, etc.).
- Reverse roles and repeat.

This can be linked and extended with the topic on Birthdays.

◆ SEE PAGE 59

Activities can also be linked to Action Rhymes on clothes and weather. Suggested rhymes are *Here we go round the mulberry bush* and *Incey Wincey Spider*.

◆ SEE PAGES 31 AND 33

8 Making children's personal records

Children in any school environment are individuals and are progressing at different rates of development. Whatever level they reach, it is important to help them to assess their development either physically, socially, intellectually or emotionally. Here are three examples of personal records in the form of charts.

Chart 1: a growth chart: *How tall are you?*

Chart 2: a behaviour chart. ◆ SEE PHOTOCOPIABLE PAGE 6

Chart 3: a progress chart: *I can …* ◆ SEE PHOTOCOPIABLE PAGES 7 AND 8

Why use children's personal records?

These sorts of records or charts can be used in topic work 'About myself'. The pedagogical aims behind using these charts in class are to:

… encourage children to develop a sense of achievement
… develop a positive attitude to work
… help children see progress in their physical and emotional development as well as their progress in learning English
… encourage children to express their worries or concerns
… help the teacher monitor and assess the development of the child.

The linguistic aims are to teach vocabulary in the four areas of a child's personal development: physical, social, emotional and intellectual.

Lexis: *centimetres, 1 metre, numbers 1-100.*

Questions : *How tall are you? Who is the tallest? (Find someone who is …) Which is the longest?*

Comparisons: *tall, taller, tallest; long, longer, longest; short, shorter, shortest.*

Behaviour: *good, bad.*

Progress: *I can … now.*

How to make and use a growth chart

1 Basic procedure

Materials needed: long strips of paper, 10cm longer than the tallest child in the class; sticky labels; crayons; a measuring stick.

- Find space on the door or classroom wall. Mark a strip in one-centimetre intervals up to 1 metre 50cm and stick it to the wall.
- Using L1, ask the children to come out in pairs to be measured in height. Each child measures their partner, then changes over to be measured.
- Ask *How tall are you?* Help children to reply *I am … centimetres tall.*
- Show them how to measure a strip of paper to the same length as their height and to cut the strip at this point. Tell them to put their names on the strips.
- Stick each strip to the wall securely. Do not arrange the strips in any order.
- To compare heights, as they cannot see the tops of their heads, they can draw a nose on the strip where their nose comes to, and then compare how tall they are against another child's strip.

2 Extension activity using the growth chart

- Look at the chart on the classroom wall. Ask the class *Who is the tallest? Which is the longest strip?*
- Point to the longest strip and read the name.
- Say *X is the tallest.* Tell the children to repeat.
- Ask the children to find someone in the class who is nearly the same height as them. They must ask *How tall are you?*
- When they have found that person, tell them to come out to the chart and measure themselves against the other strip of paper.
- Higher-level students can find the difference in the height of the tallest and the shortest person.

How to make and use a personal behaviour chart

When a child is not happy at school they sometimes need extra attention and can often cause problems in the classroom. It is not always possible in large classes to spend a lot of extra time with them. When a child changes in behaviour, it may help the teacher to see why this happens and to assist in any problems. It may be necessary to use L1 before translating into English. Before starting any form of behaviour programme it is necessary for the children to understand what is good and bad behaviour. Having established your expectations in class, you can reinforce them with a personal behaviour chart.

1 Basic procedure

Materials needed: one sheet of A4 paper for each child or a copy of the chart on PHOTOCOPIABLE PAGE 6.

- Give the children time to copy the chart from the board, or make photocopies of the chart and give them one each.
- When they have drawn the chart, explain to the children how to fill in the symbols.
- This can be done daily with an appropriate facial expression. The faces can be made to look like a dog or rabbit, as preferred.
- The chart is usable for four weeks. It is best for the teacher to review the chart at the end of each week or sooner if there are some problems.
- At the end of the four-week period you will have evidence of how often the child did not manage the expected behaviour and if there are any sessions or times of the week that they find particularly difficult.
- It may be necessary to consult the parents if the behaviour pattern does not improve.

How to make and use a personal progress chart

1 Basic aims and procedure

Lexis: *I can ...*, *I am (not) good at ...*, future tense: *going to*, present perfect: *have learned*, revision of previous work.

Materials needed: one sheet of A4 paper per child or copies of PHOTOCOPIABLE PAGES 7 AND 8; coloured pens or pencils.

- The children can copy the chart from the board or you can make photocopies of the chart. This can be given out at the beginning of term.
- Explain to the class that they are going to keep a record of what they do in their English lessons.
- At regular intervals, discuss with the children what they can do or say in English and go through the list of functions or lexical areas on PHOTOCOPIABLE PAGE 7 with them. They colour in the circles when they know or can use the function/lexis. Alternatively, you could produce a more personalised chart for your class by erasing the six areas and writing in those you are studying.
- Give them a copy each of PHOTOCOPIABLE PAGE 8 and tell them to put the correct number in the octopus's legs.
- The list of functions/lexis can be extended to fit the legs.
- At the end of term, tell them to fill in the sentences to record what they have learned and what they are going to do next term.

Adapting for higher levels

For coursebook identification choose a page which talks about the future tense *going to*. Then discuss with the class what they want to do next term.

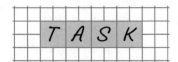

Adapt PHOTOCOPIABLE PAGES 7 AND 8 to suit your teaching schedule for the next few weeks. Try out the activity in class.

CHAPTER 5

Simple topic work

Topic work gives the following opportunities.

- For children to use language in a genuine context and to use language to reflect areas of genuine interest for their age group. For most children language is the currency of action.

- To give meaning and purpose to activities so that children can see and understand the reasons for what they are doing. They use language with a specific purpose – to communicate, persuade or find solutions, to find out and share information.

- To nurture a child's interest in the world about them. Topic activities reflect the child's natural willingness to experiment and explore. Children respond well to activities which are meaningful and relevant.

- To add more depth and variety to language learning than coursebooks can provide.

- To reflect and compliment other areas of the learning curriculum. Topic work can link target language and activities to other areas of the child's learning experience. In this way the activities they undertake in their English class can become a passport to increasing general knowledge and finding out.

- To provide a genuine purpose for inter-pupil communication.

Topic 1: Birthdays

Aims of the topic

Children's birthdays are an opportunity for celebration in the classroom. For children they are very important occasions. It is a useful way of helping children to learn and remember their birthday date and the months of the year. It is also useful for teaching the ordinals 1st to 31st.

Linguistic aims: to teach vocabulary about birthdays, days of the week, months of the year, feelings, parts of the body, shapes, food.

Topic lexis: *birthday party, feeling happy, invitations, friends,* dates, days of the week, months of the year, *parcel, presents.*

Questions: *How old are you? How are you feeling? Are you feeling …? Who has a birthday today? Can you come to my party?*

Verbs: *to clap, to stamp, to nod, to wave, to shout, to know.*

Feelings: *happy, sad, angry, nervous, afraid.*

Parts of the body: *feet, head, hands.*

Shapes: *square, round, long, thin, fat.*

Food: *cakes, sausages, crisps, drinks, orange juice, Coca-Cola.*

Preparation

1 Action song

◆ SEE PAGE 23

● This is an action song which is often sung at birthday parties in the UK.
  <u>Verse 1</u>

  If you're 'happy and you 'know it, clap your 'hands,
  If you're 'happy and you 'know it, clap your 'hands,
  If you're 'happy and you 'know it
  And you 'want us all to 'show it,
  If you're 'happy and you 'know it, clap your 'hands!

  Verse 2: If you're 'happy and you 'know it, stamp your 'feet, etc.
  Verse 3: … nod your 'head, etc.
  Verse 4: … wave your 'hands, etc.
  Verse 5: … shout We 'are!, etc.

● Write the words of the song on the board or copy them out before the lesson and give each child a photocopy. Read the song to the children and then read the song together. Do the actions with each verse.

● Divide the class into four groups. Group 1 sings Verse 1 twice and does the actions. Group 2 sings Verse 2 twice and does the actions. Group 3 sings Verse 3 twice and does the actions. Group 4 sings Verse 4 twice and does the actions. The whole class joins in the last verse.

● Give each group a different verse and repeat, with them singing each verse only once this time.

2 Talking about feelings

● Talk about feelings in L1. Ask the children *How are you feeling today?* Draw seven circles on the board, add the expressions, and put the words *happy*, *sad*, *angry*, *afraid*, *tired*, *hungry* and *thirsty* underneath.

● Point to each picture. Mime these feelings and say *I am feeling …* today. Point to the pictures again and ask the class to repeat after you and mime the feelings.

● Ask the children to work in pairs, A and B. Child A chooses to mime one of the feelings and asks *How am I feeling?* Child B must guess and say *You are feeling …* Change the roles and repeat.

3 Class activity: What do you want for your birthday?

- Talk about birthday presents and what the children want for their birthdays (you can do this in L1). Write up a list of the presents they mention on the board. Add a small drawing of each one if you can.

- Ask the children to work in pairs again. Child A asks *What do you want for your birthday?* and Child B replies *I want a …*

4 Class activity: What shape is the parcel?

- Draw a picture of different shapes of boxes on the board, e.g. big and square, long and thin, small, round and fat.

- Point to each shape and ask *What shape is this parcel?* Answer *This parcel is big and square/long and thin, etc.* Repeat the question and ask the children to draw a picture of a parcel, colour it in and decorate it.

- Ask the children to say the shapes together with you. Tell the children to work in pairs. Child A asks *What shape is this parcel?* and Child B replies *This parcel is …* Let them change roles and repeat the question.

Adapting for higher levels

Higher-level students can extend the activity by asking more questions, e.g. *Who is this present for? It's for Mum. It's for Dad,* etc.

- Put the pictures of the parcels on the wall in a large pile and label the picture *What is in the presents?*

Presentation and practice

1 Party game: Pass the parcel

This is a traditional game that British children play at parties. In preparation for the lesson, you'll need some strips of plain paper, some wrapping paper and SELLOTAPE, and some sweets. First write ten questions or instructions on the strips of paper, e.g.

> 1 What is your name?

> 2 How old are you?

> 3 Go and touch the door.

> 4 What colour is the floor?

> 5 Where is the parcel?

> 6 Whose birthday is it today?

> 7 Count up to twenty.

> 8 What day is it today?

> 9 When is your birthday?

> 10 What do you want for your birthday?

Wrap up one of the sweets in the wrapping paper with one of the questions and stick the paper down firmly. Continue to add one sweet and a question strip inside a layer of wrapping paper until all the questions have been used up. The parcel is now ready for the game.

- Ask the children to sit in a circle on the floor of the classroom, gym or outside in the playground. Show them the parcel. Play some music on a cassette recorder, pass the parcel to the first child and show the children how to pass it on. The game works best if the children can't see you operating the cassette recorder!

- Stop the music and explain that the child who is holding the parcel can take off one sheet of paper very carefully. When they have taken off one sheet, ask them *What is inside the parcel?* Ask them to read the question and to give the right answer. If they are correct they have the sweet. If the answer is wrong, they must pass it to the next child, who must read the question and if correct, then they can continue the game.

- Start the music again, let the children pass the parcel round, and stop as before. The child holding the parcel can take off another layer of wrapping, and answer the question. When all the paper has been taken off the parcel the game is finished.

Adapting for higher levels

Make the questions or instructions more difficult, e.g. *Where do you live? Go to the front of the class and sing a song. Run around the circle and touch the floor. Hop on one leg ten times*, etc.

2 Make an invitation to a birthday party

- This activity practises *Please come to my party*, prepositions: *on* (dates), *at* (place/time), addresses, *Where do you live?* The children will need half a sheet of A4 card, coloured felt tip pens or pencils.

- Write up the invitation on the board. Ask the children to fold the card in half and to decorate and colour the cover. They then copy the words from the board onto the inside of the card clearly and neatly, and fill in the missing information. Ask each child to write the name of a friend on their invitation.

To: _____ (your friend's name)

🎈 **Please come to my party** 🎈

On: _____ (day/date)

_____

At: _____ (time)

_____

At: _____ (place)

_____

From: _____ (your name)

- A classroom post box can be made from a large cardboard box. Seal the top of the box and cut a rectangular hole 30cm by 10cm in the top. The children can post their invitations and send them to someone in the same class. Choose a child to be the postman/woman to deliver the cards to the other children.

3 Making a birthday chart

For this activity you'll need a large sheet of card or stiff paper, coloured felt tip pens, strips of paper the size of each rectangle, BLU-TACK or SELLOTAPE. Look at PHOTOCOPIABLE PAGE 9. If your photocopier can enlarge to A3, make a copy on the machine. If not, copy the chart by hand onto the large sheet of card or paper. This has the advantage that you can make it bigger than A3. Write the children's names on the strips of paper or the children can write their own. These can be stuck on with BLU-TACK or SELLOTAPE to show when all the children's birthdays are.

4 Using the birthday chart: months and dates

To teach the months of the year and saying the date. ◆ SEE PAGES 55 AND 56

- Use the birthday chart to practice dates and to teach questions like *When is your birthday? Which month is it? What date is it?* and the answer *My birthday is on/in …* This also gives useful practice in pronouncing the *th* in ordinals. In case any of the children are uncertain when their birthday is, have a class register handy.

- Ask the children *When's your birthday?* Say *My birthday's in (November).* Point to the (November) column.

- Ask the children *What day/date is your birthday?* Say *My birthday's on the (11th).* Point to number (11). Then write your name on a strip of paper, put it on the chart and say *My birthday's on November 11th.* Tell the children to say with you *Your birthday's on November 11th.*

- Choose one child who has a birthday today or recently. Ask *When's your birthday?* If the child answers correctly, they can write their name on a strip of paper and put it on the chart.

- Tell the children to work in pairs and ask each other *When's your birthday?* and reply *My birthday's on …* They can then write their names on the strips of paper and stick them on the birthday chart.

- The children can count how many birthdays there are in each month and see which has the least and the most.

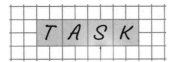

Which of these activities would you use for a birthday party in your country or the country where you are teaching? How would you adapt them?

Topic 2: Festivals

Identify festivals that the children especially enjoy, e.g. carnivals and celebrations such as Christmas or other religious festivals. Bear these in mind when you read through the following activities. Note that birthdays are dealt with as a separate topic on pages 59-63.

Aims of the topic

Why use festival activities with your class?

● For motivation. Festivals are traditionally a time when everybody joins together and participates in shared celebrations.

● Children have a very positive attitude towards festivals.

● For topical relevance. These values and celebrations can be reflected in the English classroom too and, if the children are excited about a local festival, it is nice to be able to reflect this.

● For interest. It is a good opportunity for bringing English class activities closer to the children's world, interest and activity.

● For tolerance. Festival activities provide us with an opportunity for cross-cultural awareness (an awareness of shared cultural history, of things that are different from one country to another).

● For variety. Festival activities broaden the use of English, taking it beyond the confines of language contained or generated in a coursebook.

You can use other chapters in this book to explore the topic of Festivals. This will allow you the flexibility to use the topic area in a way that is integrated and familiar with other areas of classroom activity. It also allows for a shortage of time, giving simple ideas that can be dipped into, but do not need to take up a lot of class time.

Using other chapters in this book for festival activities

If you do not have much class time to dedicate to the theme of festivals, you could integrate it with other areas of class activity. This would allow you to recognise and touch upon the theme, without having to dedicate more than one or two lessons to it.

1 Personal scrapbooks ◆ PAGES 43–46

Here are some ideas for using the children's personal scrapbooks to include festival activities. The children can:

… design a costume for the festival you are focusing on. They could invent a character of their own, or they might like to pretend to be a fictional character from a traditional story, such as *Cinderella*, *Puss in Boots*, *Little Red Riding Hood*, *Goldilocks and the Three Bears*, etc.

… bring in photographs of festival celebrations.

… use magazines and to cut out pictures of famous people. They can then cut out different bodies and stick them together, making a festival collage.

Adapting for older children

Older children could label or write a description of the festival costume, photographs or picture collages.

2 Personal dictionaries ◆ PAGES 40–42

If you have opted for a personal dictionary organised according to topic, the children can use two pages of their dictionary and write the heading *Festivals*. Words you might want to include are: *carnival, party, procession, music, party games, mask, musical instruments* and characters' names.

3 Class noticeboard ◆ PAGES 46–49

Here are some ideas for using the class noticeboard to include festival activities.

- Stick up any of the things that the children have made during the festival activities, such as making carnival masks or a festival poster.

- Stick up pictures from magazines or photos and write labels in English, e.g. *This is a carnival procession in Tenerife. This girl is dancing. This man is playing a drum. This is a cake for* (name of festival).

4 Instant puppets ◆ PAGES 49–51

You can use the instant puppets to include festival activities. The children can make a festival character puppet and use the puppets to act out ROLEPLAY dialogues from the coursebook you are using or to act out the festival rhyme on PAGE 67. They could also use instant puppets to act out the story behind a religious festival, e.g. Christmas.

5 Masks ◆ PAGES 51–54

You can use masks to include festival activities. The children can make a festival mask and then use the masks to act out or adapt dialogues from your coursebook or to act out the festival rhyme on PAGE 67. Use the masks to play the festival party games.

6 Making flashcards ◆ PAGES 38–39

Here are some ideas for FLASHCARDS that you might like to make to reflect the festival theme: party, procession, music, party games, mask, musical instruments and characters' names, names of special foods eaten at festival times. Play either of the FLASHCARD games to practice this lexis. ◆ PAGE 17

7 Adapting games

Here are some ideas for how to adapt some of the games presented in this book.

<u>What's missing?</u> ◆ PAGE 11

Play the game by writing festival words on the board. Ask the children to memorise them and to close their eyes. Rub one word off the board and ask the children to tell you which word is missing. Repeat this process until all the words are gone.

<u>Buzz!</u> ◆ PAGE 12

Play this game using festival characters and instructions. Get each child to think of a character they want to be. Play the game in the following way: Child A says their character, e.g. *I'm a clown.* Child B then points to Child A and says *She's a clown. And I'm a king.* Child C then points to A and B and says *She's a clown. He's a king and I'm a ghost.* Child D should then say *Buzz!* A variation on this game would be for Child D to give the three preceding children an instruction to carry out, saying *Clown, king, ghost. Stand up.*

<u>The 'Pen' game</u> ◆ PAGE 14

A variation on this game would be to use festival words as the starting word, e.g.

C	A	R	N	I	V	A	L
a	p	o	o	c	i	n	i
r	p	a	s	e	o	t	o
	l	d	e	c	l		n
	e			r	i		
				e	n		
				a			
				m			

<u>Consequences</u> ◆ PAGE 15

Play consequences, basing the written descriptions or the drawing activity on festival characters.

<u>The 'Yes/No' game</u> ◆ PAGE 21

Play this game using questions about the festival you are focusing on.

<u>Cat and mouse</u> ◆ PAGE 22

Play this game adapting the characters who try to find each other. Use characters associated with the festival you are focusing on.

Festival projects and activities: Party games

Here are some suggestions for games that British children play at parties. They might be nice for you to include in class activity at festival times.

1 Pass the parcel

● Follow the instructions for this from PAGE 61, but for this game make these slight changes. Wrap up a bag of sweets that the children can share as the prize for this game. Write ten messages on slips of paper, containing tasks for the children to carry out, e.g. stand up; sing a song (or part of a song); count from ten to one; stand up, turn around and sit down; say a chant; mime an action; mime an animal; go to the door; ask a friend *How old are you?*; mime a sport. Then wrap up the parcel ten more times and each time you wrap it up, put in one of the messages.

- If you do not want the children in your class to have to read the instructions, you could write a list and give the instructions verbally to the children each time they unwrap a layer of paper.
- Ask the children to sit in a circle at the front of the class. Play the game as on PAGE 62, but with the children doing the relevant task each time a layer of wrapping is removed. When the last wrapper is taken off, all the children have a sweet from the packet.

2 Musical statues

This is another traditional game that British children play at parties. If the children have made festival puppets, let them use them for this game.

- Ask the children to stand up. Explain to them, in L1, that they are going to listen to some music. While the music is playing they should dance, playing with their puppets. When the music stops everybody should stand as still as a statue. They should also hold their puppets up in the air. Anybody who moves, or moves their puppet will have to carry out a simple task.
- Ideas for tasks are as follows: jump three times; clap four times; count from ten to twenty; say *Hello* to another puppet; say a chant; mime an action; mime an animal; go to the window; ask a friend *How many brothers and sisters have you got?*; mime a sport.

Festival projects and activities: Festival poster

- Divide the class into groups of four. Give each group a large piece of paper, and some old magazines if you have them available (although this is not necessary). Ask the children to get out their coloured pencils, rulers and scissors. Tell each group to make a poster advertising a festival for their school.
- Ask the children to tell you the things they would like to include and then write the phrases on the board, in English, for the children to copy.
- You might want to follow a theme, such as fairytale characters, or Festivals around the world.
- Let the children draw pictures, cut out pictures from magazines and write on their poster. When they are finished, put the posters up in your classroom and around your school if possible.

Festival projects and activities: Festival rhyme

Ask the each child to think of a festival character. They could use their festival puppets or festival masks, if you have made them. Use the following action rhyme, substituting the name of the festival and any characters associated with the festival for the different verses. You could get the children to think of more actions to carry out.

Verse 1

It's (festival) time.
Let's all play.
(Character) and (Character) jump this way.

Verse 2: … walk this way.
Verse 3: … hop this way.
Verse 4: … clap this way.

TASK

Look back at the ideas contained in this section. Think about how the different ideas could be adapted to different festival occasions.

CHAPTER 6

Class surveys

In this chapter you will find different ideas to develop when carrying out surveys. There are different types of survey activities. All the ideas here can be used with large or small classes. Each survey idea is designed to last for one lesson of between 45 and 60 minutes.

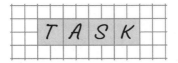

Think of three reasons why children enjoy carrying out survey activities and why they are a useful classroom activity to develop. Then compare your answers with the ideas outlined below.

"What are the benefits of using class surveys in the language classroom?"

- Surveys provide a genuine context for information exchange between pupils.
- They give the children an opportunity for ordered activity that is not desk based.
- They allow the children to express their personal opinion, or to give real information about themselves.
- They help to build a sense of class identity, building a profile of the class members.
- They are an opportunity to explore cross-curricular themes.
- They are an opportunity to explore themes of social relevance.
- They are an activity where all children can participate successfully and can work very well in mixed-ability situations.
- They are a motivating and stimulating activity and the results can be displayed in a manner that is both visually attractive and satisfying for the children who have participated.

1 Collaborative class surveys

The following survey ideas are collaborative activities where the responses of the whole class are collected to make a survey display. They are easy to adapt to reflect the language presented in your coursebook and they can be used to focus a variety of question and answer forms.

Example language focus of collaborative surveys

- *What's your favourite colour? My favourite colour's ...*
  What's your favourite football team/sport/food/toy/animal/school subject?
- *Who's your favourite pop star/sports star? My favourite ...'s ...*
- *What colour eyes have you got? I've got ... eyes.*
- *What colour hair/shoes/jumper, etc. have you got?*

Adapting for higher levels

- *How many times do you ... a day/a week/a year? I ... times a day/a week/ a year.*

- *How often do you eat chocolate/play sport/do homework/help at home/brush your teeth/bath/go on holiday/go to the swimming pool, etc.*
- *How do you go to school? I go by/on ...*
- *How many people are there in your family? There are ... people in my family.*
- *Do you live in a house or a flat? I live in a ...*

Displaying the surveys

For each of the following survey ideas you need a sheet of A4 paper for each child with a circle on it of approximately 16cm in diameter (or rectangles as shown below). You also need a large sheet of paper on which to mount the survey display. Here are some ideas for ways of displaying the information.

Lesson plan 1

Language focus of this survey

Use this survey idea to practise different lexical areas, e.g. *What's your favourite ...?*, substituting the appropriate FOCUS QUESTION according to what you want to practise.

Basic procedure

1 Lexis revision

Choose one of the 10-minute games in CHAPTER 1 to focus on the lexical area you want to use with this survey. Play the game with the children.

2 Survey chant

Say a simple chant with the children to practise the language structures they need to carry out the survey. Say the following chant twice. The first time the children listen. The second time they clap the rhythm. Say the chant one more time and encourage the children to join in.

What's your
What's your
What's your favourite (colour)?
What's your
What's your
What's your favourite (colour)?

Try to elicit the response from the class. See if anybody knows how to say *My favourite (colour's ...).*

3 Personalisation of the survey chant

Say the chant again with the whole class. As you all chant the last line, point to a child and encourage them to tell everybody their favourite (colour).

4 Collaborative activity: answering the question

- Ask the children to get out scissors and coloured pencils. Give each child in the class a circle. Encourage the children to ask their neighbour *What's your favourite (colour)?* Tell the neighbour to answer the question using *My favourite (colour's)* ... Repeat this process until everybody has had a chance to ask and answer. You could do this as a chain activity.

- Tell the children to colour in the circle to record their answer, using their favourite colour. When everybody has recorded their answer get the children to write their name in the circle and to then cut out their circle. These can then be used to form a survey display by sticking them in groups on a large piece of paper. (Alternatively, children could colour in a number of circles, then write their names on the colour they like best, as in the illustration on the previous page.)

5 Language follow-up

You might like to ask the some comprehension questions, e.g. *What's Marta's favourite (colour)? How many boys like (colour) best? How many children like (colour) best?*

Adapting for higher levels

Higher-level students could write about the survey. They could either answer the above questions or follow a pattern such as *In our class ten children like (colour) best.* This personalisation writing activity could be carried out in the children's personal scrapbooks. ◆ SEE PAGES 43–46

6 Writing option

You could ask each child to write one sentence about the results of the survey. These could then be stuck around the edge of the survey display.

Lesson plan 2
Language focus of this survey

Use this survey idea to practise different lexical areas and substitute the appropriate FOCUS QUESTION, e.g. *What colour ... have you got? How many times do you ... a day/a week/a year? Do you live in a house or a flat?*

Basic procedure

1 Lexis revision

As Lesson plan 1.

2 Structure anagram

Write an anagram on the board of the structure you want to practise with the class, e.g.

many   do   How   times   chocolate   eat   week   ?   a   you
= How many times a week do you eat chocolate?

Put in the capital letter and question mark. This will help the children to identify the first and last word in the question. Write up the answer and rub out the anagram. Read the question with the whole class. Then ask individual children to give you their answer.

3 Collaborative activity: answering the question

As Lesson plan 1, substituting the relevant FOCUS QUESTION, e.g. *What colour …
have you got?* Tell the children to use the circle to record their answer as before.
You can do this in the following ways.

- *What colour …?* – as in Lesson plan 1.
- *My favourite … is … /I've got … /I live in a …* – the children can draw a
  picture of their answer.
- *I … times a day/a week/a year* – the children can draw a number which
  represents how many times they carry out the action.

When everybody has recorded their answer tell the children to write their name
in the circle and to then cut out their circle. These can then be used to form a
survey display.

4 Language follow-up

As Lesson plan 1.

2 Transfer surveys: graphs

These are two-stage surveys where the children ask their classmates a question
and record their answers on a chart. The information they have collected can
then be transferred to a different visual representation. Each child will have their
own results. It is easy to adapt to a variety of lexical areas of interest to the
children. To adapt this survey idea to practise different lexical areas and
structures, substitute the appropriate FOCUS QUESTION. You can choose whether to
do this survey with the whole class or in smaller groups. You also need squared
paper for the children to transfer the information.

**Example language focus
of these surveys**

- *When's your birthday? My birthday's in …*
- *What's your favourite football team/sport/food/toy/animal?*
- *What time do you go to bed/get up/have lunch/have dinner/leave for school?*

Lesson plan 3

1 Lexis revision

Find a 10-minute game that can be used to revise the lexical area you want to
focus on. Then play it with your class.

◆ SEE PAGES 9–17

2 Mingle activity

Ask the children to write the month of their birthday on a piece of paper. Tell
the children to stand up and move around the class. When you clap your
hands and say *Stop* they should ask the person nearest to them *When's your
birthday?* If the children have the same birthday month they should stay
together and move around the class. To get the children to sit down say *Sit
down March/July,* etc.

3 Preparing the survey chart

Give each pupil a copy of PHOTOCOPIABLE PAGE 10. Then explain to the children that they have to ask different people in the class the FOCUS QUESTION. They should put a tick or a cross in the corresponding square on the grid.

When's your birthday?

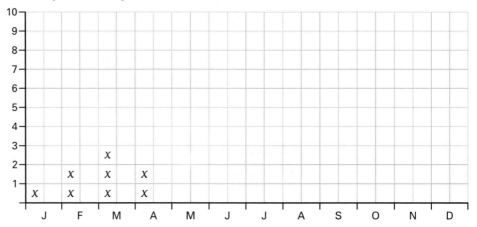

4 Carrying out the survey as a whole class

Ask the children to get out a pencil and to take their chart. Divide the class into two groups, A and B. Instruct each group to stand in a line facing the other group (as in 1 in the diagram). Tell the children in Group A to ask the person standing opposite them the FOCUS QUESTION and to record his/her answer, then to answer B's question. Divide each group into two (AX, AY, BX, BY, as in 2 in the diagram) and repeat this process. Keep splitting the groups so that all the children have swapped questions and answers in the end.

5 Carrying out the survey in groups

Ask the children to get out a pencil and to take their chart. Divide the class into four groups. Encourage the children to ask their group members the FOCUS QUESTION and to record their answer on their chart.

6 Transferring the information

Give each child a piece of squared paper. Show the children how to make their graph. Draw a simple version on the board as follows.

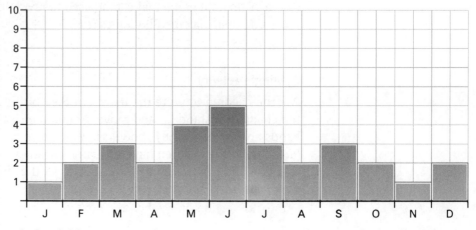

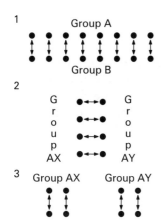

Ask the children to count how many answers were the same for each category. They should then colour in the number of squares.

7 Displaying the children's work

The results of this survey could be stuck into the children's personal scrapbooks.
◆ SEE PAGES 43–46

Adapting for higher levels

Higher-level children could write about the survey. They could either answer the above questions or follow a pattern such as *Ten children have their birthday in July. There are six birthdays in May.*

3 Transfer surveys: Venn diagrams

These are two-stage surveys where the children ask their classmates a question and record their answers on a chart. The information they have collected can then be transferred to a different visual representation. It is easy to adapt to a variety of lexical areas of interest to the children. You need one copy of PHOTOCOPIABLE PAGE 11 for each child. You also need a large sheet of paper on which to mount the results of the survey. You can choose whether to do this survey with the whole class or in smaller groups.

Example language focus of these surveys

- *Have you got a (cat)? Yes, I have./No, I haven't.*
- *Can you swim/speak English/ride a horse/skateboard, etc?*

Lesson plan 4

1 Lexis revision

Find a 10-minute game that can be used to revise the lexical area you want to focus on. Then play it with your class.
◆ SEE PAGES 9–17

2 Blackboard practice

- Draw four large sections on the board, as this example.

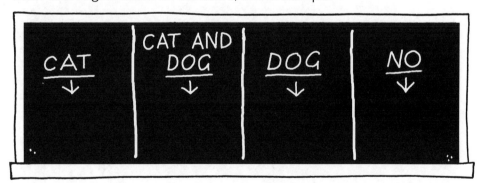

- Ask the children to stand up. Ask them a question, e.g. *Have you got a dog?* If their answer is *Yes*, they should come and stand under the 'dog' section on the board. Repeat this process for *Have you got a cat?* Then ask all the children who have both pets to move to the 'cat and dog' section. Ask the remaining children the question, and if they say *No* ask them to stand under the 'no' section on the board. Then ask everybody to sit down.

3 Preparing the survey chart

● Brainstorm the vocabulary from the lexical area that you want to practise with the class. If you want to practise animal words, ask the children to tell you as many as they can. Make a list of these words, adding any extra ones the children have not thought of.

● Assign two words to each child. If you want, the children can also work in pairs. In this case you would give one copy of the Venn diagram to each pair of children. Ask the children to fill in the words that they are going to ask about. Write them on the board for the children to copy, or get them to copy them from the coursebook.

● Then explain to the children that they have to ask different people in the class the FOCUS QUESTION. They should write their name in the corresponding section of the chart, e.g.

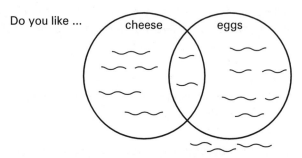

Do you like ...

4 Carrying out the survey as a whole class

Ask the children to get out a pencil and give them each a copy of PHOTOCOPIABLE PAGE 11. Divide the class into two groups. Follow the instructions in point 4 on PAGE 72 for a whole-class survey.

5 Carrying out the survey in groups

Ask the children to get out a pencil and to take their Venn diagram. Divide the class into four groups. Tell the children to ask their group members the FOCUS QUESTION and to record their answer on the Venn diagram.

6 Displaying the children's work

The results of this survey can be used to form a class display.

Food Survey

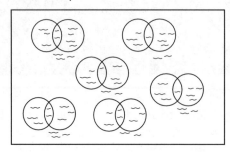
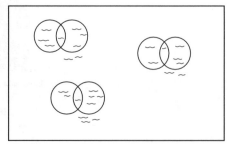

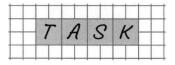

Look at the language focus possibilities outlined in each of the lesson plans. Then identify where the surveys could be used to reflect the content of your coursebook.

CHAPTER 7

Story activities

The activities described in this chapter are designed to be flexible enough to use and adapt with a range of traditional stories. They use repetitive language patterns and can be adapted to practise a range of language points.

"Why use story activities with your class?"

There are a number of reasons for using stories in the language classroom.

- For motivation. Most children enjoy having stories read to them, or reading stories for themselves.
- To practise different skills. They are a good reading and writing starting point. They provide an opportunity for children to make their own books. They provide drama and ROLEPLAY opportunities. They practise and reinforce lexis and structures, and develop conceptual skills such as prediction, guessing the meaning of new words, training the memory.
- For interest. Stories can be chosen to reflect the language topic covered in the coursebook or other areas of school activity.
- For social relevance. Stories can often be used to discuss and explore issues of social relevance, e.g. an awareness of good and bad social behaviour, of emotions, of shared cultural history, of things that are different from one country to another.
- For variety. Stories broaden the use of English, taking it beyond the confines of language contained or generated in a coursebook.
- For context. Stories are a medium that the children are familiar with. They give context and meaning to the language. And the action in the story gives the children a genuine reason for listening.

"How do you choose the right kind of story?"

Look for stories that have the following elements.

- The story should have a simple storyline.
- The story should not be too long.
- The language should match (or should be easily adapted to) the pupils' level of proficiency. It should contain repetitive phrases.
- You should have a clear plan of the activities you want to use to exploit the story.
- Action stories are the easiest to exploit.
- Dialogue exchanges between characters in the story should be short and memorable.

TASK

Think of three traditional tales that the children will know. How many of them have repetitive language patterns?

Story 1: The enormous turnip

Language focus

Topic lexis: *Grandpa, Grandma, dog, cat, garden, seeds, potatoes, carrots, tomatoes, turnips, days of the week. raining, sunny, hot, vegetables, big, enormous, little, tiny, mouse, sad, happy, heavy, kitchen, delicious, soup, a bowl.*

Verbs: *to look at, to be, have got, to plant, to say, to ask, go into the …, to pull, can/can't, to move, to hide behind, to watch, to touch, to dance around, to try, to lift, to carry, to make, to give.*

Expressions: *Good idea, Let's …, What's the weather like today? Help me/us please. It's OK. Thank you.*

Other: Numbers 1, 2, 3, *every day, some, then one day, and, very, too, yes, this, everybody, now, but, together.*

Materials: If possible, draw a picture (or find an appropriate one) of Grandpa, Tom, Emma and Grandpa's dog and cat to set the scene.

Telling the story

Tell the children that you are going to tell them a story and ask them if they know the tale of *The enormous turnip*. Make sure that everybody is quiet and attentive and that they're sitting comfortably. Show them some pictures of the characters if you can.

- Read the story to the children. An alternative way to read the story to the children is to record it onto a cassette.
- Mime the actions. Use facial expression and gesture. Read at a slow, even pace. Keep eye contact with the children, as this will help to maintain their interest.
- Once you have read the story ask the children to tell you, in L1, what they think happened.
- Then read the story again, stopping after each section to ask the children to summarise what's happening.

Adapting for higher levels

For higher-level students you could tell this story using the past tense.

Checking comprehension

Ask the children some questions about the story. Try to use language that reflects the language content and level of the story.

What animals are there in the story?
What vegetables do they plant?
What's the weather like on Monday?
Are the vegetables small?
Can Grandpa pull the turnip?
Is the enormous turnip heavy?
Who makes some turnip soup?
Is the turnip soup delicious?

Lexis comprehension check

To further check or consolidate lexis comprehension, you could play a 10-minute game.

◆ SEE PAGES 9–17

The story   **Note:** The asterisks (*) in the story refer to *Making a story frieze*, ON PAGE 78.

The enormous turnip

* Look at Grandpa, Tom and Emma, Grandpa's dog and cat. They are all in Grandpa's garden. They've got some seeds.

* 'Let's plant the seeds,' says Grandpa. 'Good idea,' say Tom and Emma.

* Grandpa, Tom and Emma plant the seeds. 1, 2, 3 carrots; 1, 2, 3 potatoes; 1, 2, 3 tomatoes; 1, 2, 3 turnips.

* On Monday Tom asks, 'What's the weather like today?' 'It's raining!' say Emma and Grandpa.

* On Tuesday Tom asks, 'What's the weather like today?' 'It's raining!' say Emma and Grandpa.

* Every day Tom asks, 'What's the weather like?' and every day Emma and   Grandpa say, 'It's raining!'

* Then one day Tom asks, 'What's the weather like today?' and Emma and Grandpa say, 'It's sunny and hot. Let's look at the garden!'

* Grandpa, Tom, Emma, the dog and the cat go into the garden. They look at the vegetables.

* 'Look at the carrots. They're very big. Look at the potatoes. They're very big. Look at the tomatoes. They're very big. And look at the turnips. They're very big too.'

* 'Yes, and this turnip is enormous!' says Grandpa.

* Grandpa pulls the enormous turnip. 'Pull, pull, pull, 1, 2, 3. I can't move it. Help me please,' he says.

* Then Tom helps Grandpa. 'Pull, pull, pull, 1, 2, 3. We can't move it. Help us please, ' they say.

* Then Emma helps Grandpa. 'Pull, pull, pull, 1, 2, 3. We can't move it. Help us please, ' they say.

* Then the dog helps. 'Pull, pull, pull, 1, 2, 3. We can't move it. Help us please,' they say.

* Then the cat helps. A tiny little mouse is hiding behind the turnip. He is watching Grandpa, Tom, Emma, the dog and the cat.
'Pull, pull, pull, 1, 2, 3. We can't move it. Oh, no,' they say. Everybody's sad.

* 'It's OK,' says the tiny little mouse. 'I can help you.'

* Then everybody pulls the enormous turnip. Grandpa pulls. Tom pulls. Emma pulls. The dog pulls. The cat pulls ... and the tiny little mouse pulls, and ... 'Pull, pull, pull, 1, 2, 3. We can move it. Thank you mouse!'

* Now everybody's happy. They look at the enormous turnip. They touch the enormous turnip. * They dance round the enormous turnip. * Then they try to lift the enormous turnip. But the enormous turnip is very heavy. * Grandpa can't carry it. * Tom can't carry it. * Emma can't carry it. * The dog can't carry it. * The cat can't carry it. * The tiny little mouse can't carry it ... * But all together they **can** carry it.

* Together they carry the enormous turnip into the kitchen. * And Grandma makes some delicious turnip soup.

* Grandma gives a bowl to Grandpa. * She gives a bowl to Tom. * She gives a bowl to Emma. * She gives a bowl to the dog. * She gives a bowl to the cat.
* And she gives an enormous bowl to the tiny little mouse.

* 'Mmm. This soup is delicious. Thank you mouse' says everybody.

Miming the story

- Read the story to the children. Ask them to mime the actions and emotions as you read. Help them with the actions they should carry out.
- In large classes you could ask groups of children to come to the front and mime. The rest of the class acts as spectators.

Acting out the story

Read the story again. Ask the children to mime the story again and to chorus certain repetitive lines, e.g.

1, 2, 3 (carrots).
What's the weather like today?
'It's raining!' say Emma and Grandpa.
Look at the (carrots). They're very big.
Pull, pull, pull, 1, 2, 3. I/ We can't move it. Help me/us please.
(Grandpa) can't carry it.
Grandma gives a bowl to (Grandpa).

Making a story frieze

- Ask the children to work individually or in pairs.
- Copy the story text and cut it up into sections. There are 35 sections (marked with *), but you can divide it into fewer sections if you wish.
- Give one piece of text to each child or pair and ask the children to illustrate the text.
- Collect up the finished pictures. Put them in the order of the story and then make a story frieze.

Adapting for higher levels

If your pupils are quite confident at writing you could ask them to copy out the piece of text to accompany their pictures.

Making story puppets

- Get the children to make puppets of the characters and the enormous turnip.
- Use these puppets to act out the story.

Story 2: Chicken Licken

This story is useful for teaching the names of farm birds and can be used in conjunction with a topic about the farm and with the action song *The farmer's in his den*, using the names of birds instead of animals. ◆ SEE PAGE 23

It has rhyming names and repetitive language. It is easy to adapt for use as a class activity and to act out the dialogue with puppets or as a ROLEPLAY.

Language focus

Topic lexis: farm birds: *chicken, hen, cock, duck, goose, turkey; acorn, fox, den.*

Verbs: *went, said, played, fell, met, followed, took, ate; I'm going, it's falling, I'm coming.*

Expressions: *Good morning. Where are you going?*

Materials: You need several copies of PHOTOCOPIABLE PAGE 12. Cut out the characters, one character for each child in the class. You also need coloured pens, pencils, and a bottle cork or a nut.

The story   See activities on PAGE 80.

Chicken Licken

Once upon a time there was a chicken called Chicken Licken. One day an acorn fell on his head.

'Help! The sky is falling down,' he said. So he went to find the King.

On the way Chicken Licken met Henny Penny.

'Good morning. Where are you going?' said Henny Penny.

'The sky is falling down and I'm going to find the King,' said Chicken Licken.

'Then I am coming too!' said Henny Penny.

So Chicken Licken and Henny Penny went to find the King.

On the way Chicken Licken and Henny Penny met Cocky Locky.

'Good morning. Where are you going?' said Cocky Locky.

'The sky is falling down, and we're going to find the King,' said Chicken Licken and Henny Penny.

'Then I am coming too!' said Cocky Locky.

So Chicken Licken, Henny Penny and Cocky Locky went to find the King.

On the way Chicken Licken, Henny Penny and Cocky Locky met Ducky Lucky.

'Good morning. Where are you going?' said Ducky Lucky.

'The sky is falling down and we're going to find the King,' said Chicken Licken, Henny Penny and Cocky Locky.

'Then I am coming too!' said Ducky Lucky.

So Chicken Licken, Henny Penny, Cocky Locky and Ducky Lucky went to find the King.

On the way Chicken Licken, Henny Penny, Cocky Locky and Ducky Lucky met Goosey Loosey.

'Good morning. Where are you going?' said Goosey Loosey.

'The sky is falling down and we're going to find the King,' said Chicken Licken, Henny Penny, Cocky Locky and Ducky Lucky.

'Then I am coming too!' said Goosey Loosey.

So Chicken Licken, Henny Penny, Cocky Locky, Ducky Lucky and Goosey Loosey went to find the King.

On the way Chicken Licken, Henny Penny, Cocky Locky, Ducky Lucky and Goosey Loosey met Turkey Lurkey.

'Good morning. Where are you going?' said Turkey Lurkey.

'The sky is falling down and we are going to find the King,' said Chicken Licken, Henny Penny, Cocky Locky, Ducky Lucky and Goosey Loosey.

'Then I am coming too,' said Turkey Lurkey.

So Chicken Licken, Henny Penny, Cocky Locky, Ducky Lucky, Goosey Loosey and Turkey Lurkey went to find the King.

BUT on the way Chicken Licken, Henny Penny, Cocky Locky, Ducky Lucky, Goosey Loosey and Turkey Lurkey met Foxey Loxey!

'Good morning. Where are you going?' said Foxey Loxey.

'The sky is falling down and we're going to find the King,' said Chicken Licken, Henny Penny, Cocky Locky, Ducky Lucky, Goosey Loosey and Turkey Lurkey.

'Follow me. I know where to find the King,' said Foxey Loxey.

So Chicken Licken, Henny Penny, Cocky Locky, Ducky Lucky, Goosey Loosey and Turkey Lurkey followed Foxey Loxey.

But he didn't take them to find the King. He took them to his den.

Foxey Loxey and all the fox family ate Chicken Licken, Henny Penny, Cocky Locky, Ducky Lucky, Goosey Loosey and Turkey Lurkey for their dinner!

So Chicken Licken, Henny Penny, Cocky Locky, Ducky Lucky, Goosey Loosey and Turkey Lurkey didn't find the King to tell him that the sky was falling down.

Before you tell the story

Write the list of characters on the board: Chicken Licken, Henny Penny, Cocky Locky, Ducky Lucky, Goosey Loosey, Turkey Lurkey, Foxey Loxey. And write up the following three extracts from the story.

1 Good morning. Where are you going?

2 The sky is falling down and I'm going to find the King.

3 Then I am coming too!

Telling the story and acting it out

- Give out the copies of PHOTOCOPIABLE PAGE 12, one to each child. Talk about the colours of these birds. Ask the class to colour the birds and the fox using the correct colour. Ask the children the name of their bird. They reply *I'm a …*
- Read the story to the class using L1 to translate difficult names. Explain that *chicken* and *hen* are the same bird, but we often use *chicken* (or *chick*) to refer to a baby hen.
- Select seven children to play the characters in the story.
- Use the bottle cork or nut to throw onto the head of Chicken Licken to demonstrate the beginning of the story.
- Repeat the story.
- Henny Penny repeats the words *Good Morning. Where are you going?*
- Chicken Licken repeats the words *The sky is falling down and I'm going to find the King.*
- Henny Penny repeats the words *Then I am coming too.*
- As each character appears in the story, tell them to repeat the question *Good morning. Where are you going?*
- The remainder of the class repeats the names.
- Chicken Licken and the additional characters reply *The sky is falling down and we're going to find the King* when it is their turn.
- The new character replies *Then I am coming too.*
- Follow this pattern as the story is read.
- When Foxey Loxey appears, ask the children to follow him into the corner of the classroom.
- Repeat the story using all the characters together in groups of chickens, hens, cocks, ducks, geese and turkeys, so that all the children have a chance to act out the words.

Extension: farmyard noises game 1

SEE ACTION GAME THE CIRCUS PAGE 20
Change the circus animals to farmyard birds. As each child is chosen, he/she must make the correct noise of the farmyard bird.

A chicken cheeps, say *cheep, cheep.*
A hen clucks, say *cluck, cluck.*
A cock crows, say *cock-a doodle-doo.*
A duck quacks, say *quack, quack.*
A goose squawks, say *squawk, squawk.*
A turkey gobbles, say *gobble, gobble.*

Extension: farmyard noises game 2

- Find a large space in the playground. This must be played in the playground to avoid disturbing other classes.
- Ask every child to make the noise of one of the birds in the story.
- Tell the class to walk around the playground making the noise of their bird.
- When they find another person making the same noise they must continue to walk around together until they have found all the people who are the same character. There should be six groups at the end of the game, i.e. one group for each of the characters in the story.

Checking comprehension

Ask the children questions about the story. Try to use language that reflects the language content and level of the story.

What fell on Chicken Licken's head?
What does Chicken Licken do?
Who does she meet?
What does she say?
What do they reply?
Who do they meet?
What happens at the end of the story?

Adapting for higher levels

Ask the children if they can think of a different ending to the story, e.g. a happy ending rather than a sad one. Then compare this with other story endings, such as *Little Red Riding Hood* or stories they know.

Making a story frieze

Ask the children to draw a picture of one of the characters from the story. Stick them in the correct order on a large piece of frieze paper. It will be necessary to illustrate the story with groups of chickens, hens, cocks, ducks, geese and turkeys to use all the drawings. Ask each child to draw a speech bubble and copy the words spoken by their character, and stick it next to this bird on the frieze.

Lexis consolidation

Find a page in your coursebook which talks about a visit to the farm. Look for pictures of the birds used in the story of *Chicken Licken*.

Choose one of the stories you thought of in the last task. Make a rough lesson plan using that story. Think about the language focus, how you can tell the story and what activities you could do with the children after the story, e.g. miming or acting out the story, checking comprehension, playing a game, making a frieze or puppets.

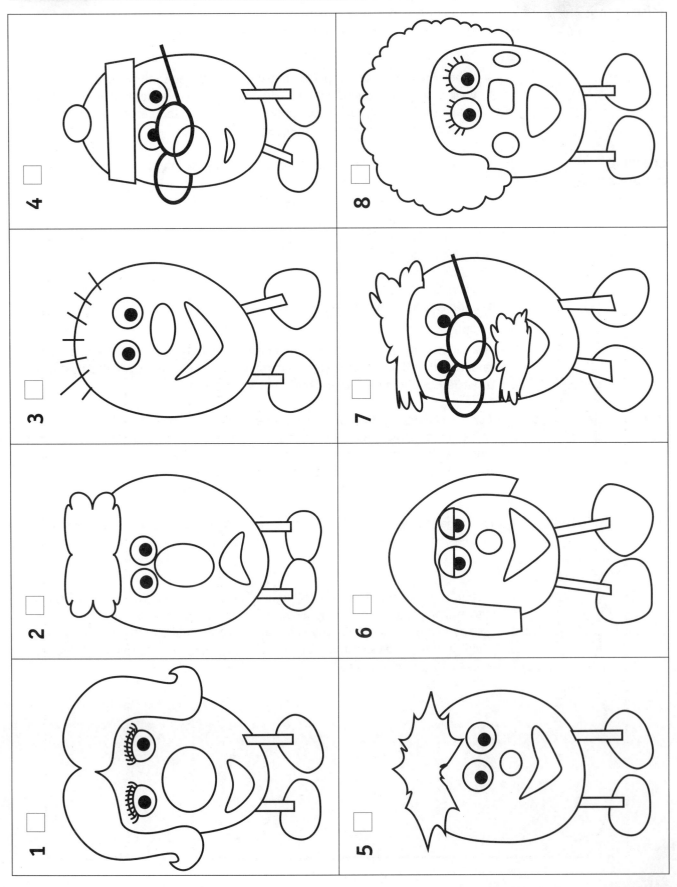

Developing Resources for Primary, © Cant & Superfine, 1997   PHOTOCOPIABLE

cut - - - - - - - - - - - - - - -

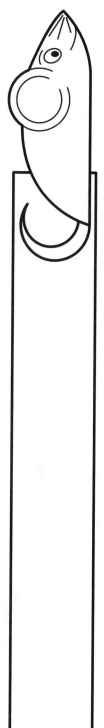

Developing Resources for Primary, © Cant & Superfine, 1997

SEE PAGE 34

Aa	Bb	Cc	Dd
Ee	Ff	Gg	Hh
Ii	Jj	Kk	Ll
Mm	Nn	Oo	Pp
Qq	Rr	Ss	Tt
Uu	Vv	Ww	
Xx	Yy	Zz	

 cold

 stormy

 windy

 foggy/misty

What's the weather like today?

MONDAY	TUESDAY	WEDNESDAY	THURSDAY	FRIDAY

This month is: ....

The temperature is: ....

This season is: ....

 snowy

 rainy/wet

 sunny/hot

 cloudy/cool

 cloudy/warm

My good behaviour chart

WEEK	MONDAY	TUESDAY	WEDNESDAY	THURSDAY	FRIDAY
1					
2					
3					
4					

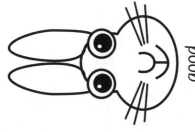 good

 not so good

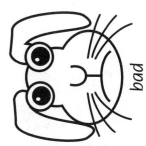 bad

My progress chart

Complete these at the end of the term.

I am good at ....

I am not good at ....

I am going to .... next.

I have learned

1 ....

2 ....

3 ....

4 ....

5 ....

Put the numbers on the octopus's legs.

1 say the numbers 1–20

2 say the days of the week

3 talk about my family

4 say the colours

5 say how old I am

6 say how tall I am

SEE PAGE 58

Developing Resources for Primary, © Cant & Superfine, 1997

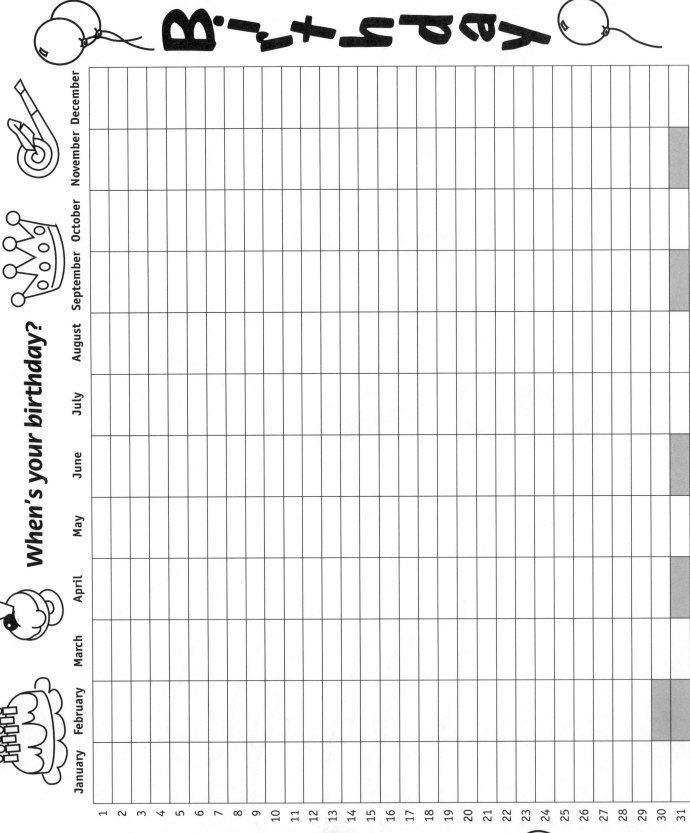

When's your birthday?

	January	February	March	April	May	June	July	August	September	October	November	December
1												
2												
3												
4												
5												
6												
7												
8												
9												
10												
11												
12												
13												
14												
15												
16												
17												
18												
19												
20												
21												
22												
23												
24												
25												
26												
27												
28												
29												
30												
31												

When's your birthday?

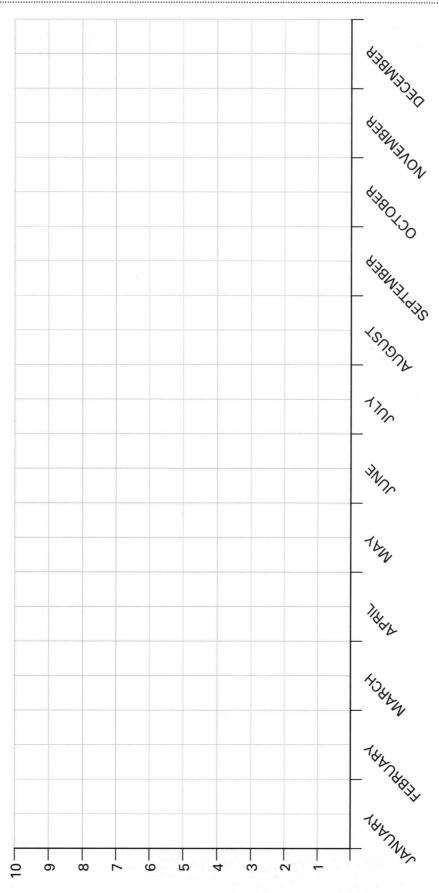

10
9
8
7
6
5
4
3
2
1

JANUARY
FEBRUARY
MARCH
APRIL
MAY
JUNE
JULY
AUGUST
SEPTEMBER
OCTOBER
NOVEMBER
DECEMBER

SEE PAGE 74

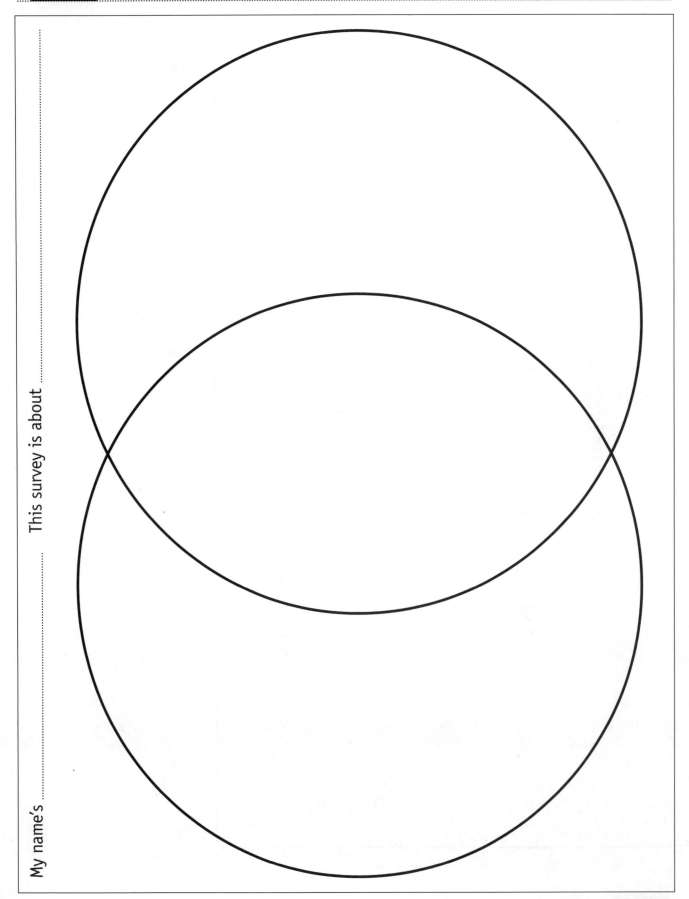

This survey is about ....

My name's ....

SEE PAGE 80

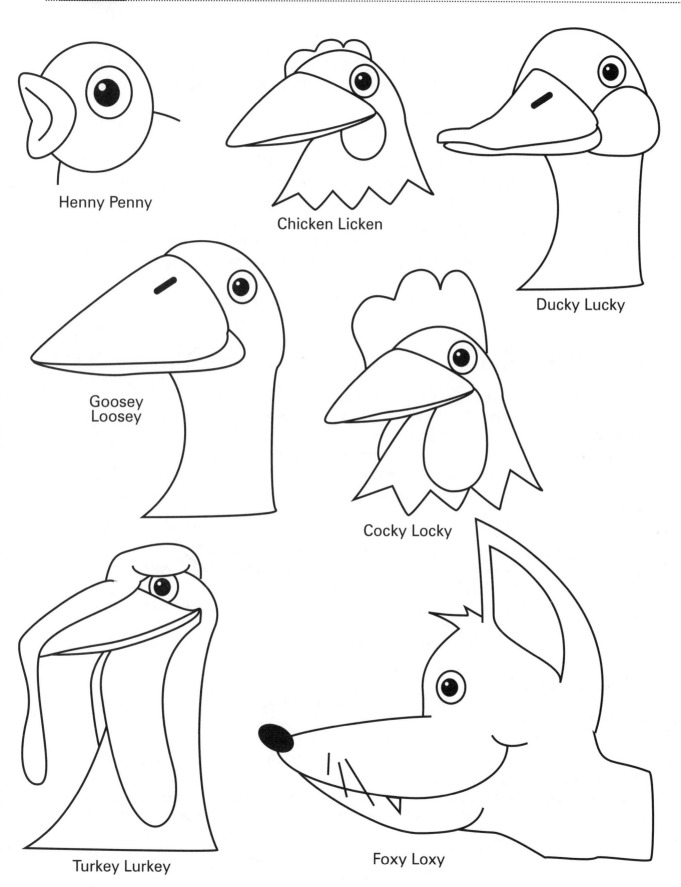

Henny Penny

Chicken Licken

Ducky Lucky

Goosey Loosey

Cocky Locky

Turkey Lurkey

Foxy Loxy

Glossary

BLU-TACK	A non-permanent sticky gum that can be used to stick paper or posters.
FLASHCARDS	These are large cards which have either a picture or a word on (sometimes both), which the teacher holds up for the class. They are often used in drills as picture/word prompts.
FOCUS LEXIS	Vocabulary items which you wish to teach or revise through a particular activity or task
FOCUS QUESTION	Questions which you use to highlight or elicit a FOCUS STRUCTURE or FOCUS LEXIS.
FOCUS STRUCTURE	Grammatical items which you wish to teach or practise through a particular activity or task.
REALIA	Real things which you can bring into class, e.g. items of clothing, toys, household items, etc., and which you can use to support the lesson.
ROLEPLAY	Any activity where pupils have to imagine themselves in a particular situation or assume particular characters.
SELLOTAPE	A sticky tape (Scotch tape) which is used to stick paper, etc.

Further reading

Brewster, J, Ellis, G and Girard, D *The Primary English Teacher's Guide* Penguin 1991
A valuable guide to teaching techniques and learning strategies for language acquisition at primary level, with many practical suggestions and lists of resources.

Brewster, J and Ellis, G *The Storytelling Handbook for Primary Teachers* Penguin 1991
This contains many practical ideas for using stories suitable for EFL.

Brumfit, C, Moon, J and Tongue, R *Teaching English to Children: from Practice to Principle* Addison Wesley Longman 1991
A thorough introduction to the background theory and practice of primary EFL. An essential for every EFL library.

Halliwell, S *Teaching English in the Primary Classroom* Addison Wesley Longman 1992
This gives theoretical and practical ideas based on good primary practice and educational theories.

House, S *An Introduction to Teaching English to Children* Richmond Publishing 1997
A thorough introduction covering the basics of teaching EFL to children, with a variety of simple activities.

Matterson, E *This Little Puffin* Puffin 1969
This is full of songs, rhymes and games for every topic and occasion, which can be used or adapted for teaching young learners of English.

Phillips, S *Young Learners* OUP 1993
This provides teachers with a good source of ideas and materials for practical activities covering all aspects of teaching EFL in the primary classroom.

Scott, W and Ytreberg, L *Teaching English to Children* Addison Wesley Longman 1990
A good resource book for classroom ideas and advice on lesson planning and management for primary EFL.

Wright, A *Storytelling with Children* OUP 1996
There are many practical ideas in this book which can be used by both inexperienced and experienced primary EFL teachers. It is an excellent resource for traditional stories and stories which can be created by the children themselves.

Index of activities

(numbers in brackets refer to photocopiable pages)

Index of structures and vocabulary

(numbers in brackets refer to photocopiable pages)

Key to Task, PAGE **17**
Whole class: 1, 2, 3, 4, 5, 7, 8, 9, 10   Groups: 1, 2, 3, 4, 5, 6, 8, 9   Fast finishers: 4, 5, 8